D1552108

198

MILITARY CONSIDERATIONS

IN CITY PLANNING: FORTIFICATIONS

PLANNING AND CITIES
(titles published to date)

PLANNING AND CITIES

General Editor

GEORGE R. COLLINS, Columbia University

MILITARY CONSIDERATIONS IN CITY PLANNING: FORTIFICATIONS

HORST DE LA CROIX

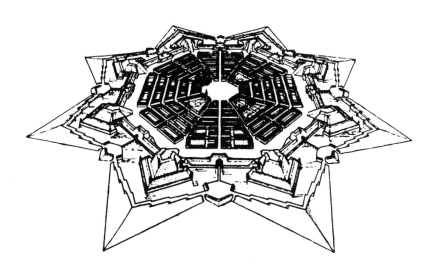

GEORGE BRAZILLER   NEW YORK

Copyright © 1972 by George Braziller, Inc.
Published simultaneously in Canada by Doubleday Canada, Limited.
All rights reserved.
For information address the publisher:
George Braziller, Inc. One Park Avenue New York, N.Y. 10016
Standard Book Number: 0-8076-0584-0 (paperbound)
                       0-8076-0585-9 (hardbound)
Library of Congress Catalog Card Number: 72-143398
Printed in the U.S.A.
First Printing

CONTENTS

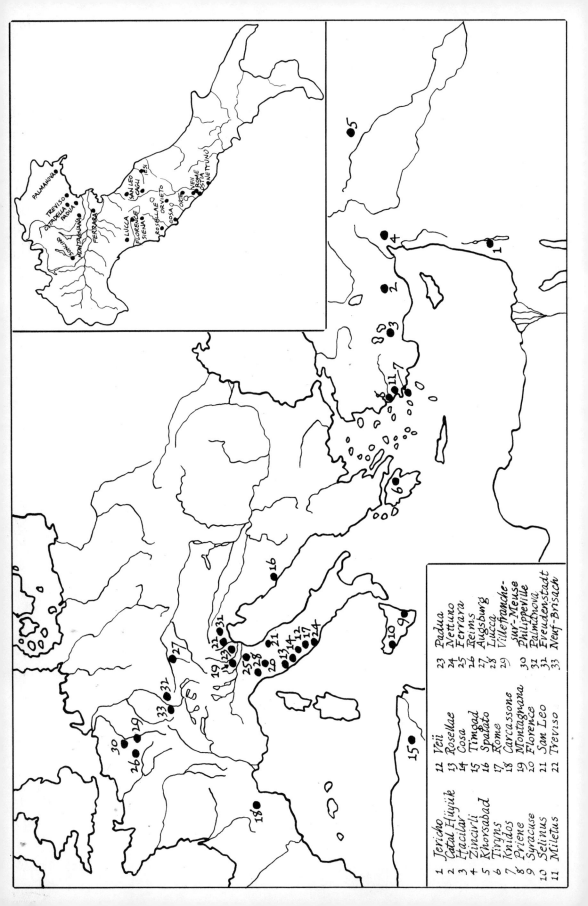

1	Jericho	12	Veii	23	Padua
2	Catal Hüyük	13	Rosellae	24	Nettuno
3	Hacilar	14	Cosa	25	Ferrara
4	Zincirli	15	Timgad	26	Reims
5	Khorsabad	16	Spalato	27	Augsburg
6	Tiryns	17	Rome	28	Lucca
7	Knidos	18	Carcassone	29	Villefranche-sur-Meuse
8	Priene	19	Montagnana	30	Philippeville
9	Syracuse	20	Florence	31	Palmanova
10	Selinus	21	San Leo	32	Freudenstadt
11	Miletus	22	Treviso	33	Neuf-Brisach

GENERAL EDITOR'S PREFACE

Throughout most of the history of civilization, the size, shape, and interior arrangements of cities have been strongly affected by man's desire to protect himself and his possessions by means of fortifications. Each advance in the technology of weapons has led to more elaborate methods of defense against them; only in the time of a powerful imperial state have individual settlements been able to grow free of ponderous wall systems.

The present author, an expert on the most intricate phase of the science of siege defense—the late Renaissance—gives us here an overview of the whole history of fortification design. His chronicle brings us up to the throttling defense systems of the late Baroque period, which were to be burst asunder by the growing range and power of offensive weapons, as well as the irresistible expansion of the nineteenth-century city, and which, in many cases, were replaced by new urban determinants: parks and boulevards (French for *bulwarks*). Interesting perspectives are cast on the conflict between military and civilian priorities in urban affairs, conflicts that are still with us although forts and armories only persist as fossils on the city scene. Because a special military vocabulary (much of it now archaic) is necessary for the description of fortifications, we have included a glossary of technical terms on p. 119 for the benefit of the reader.

This study by Horst de la Croix is the first in our series of books on Cities and Planning to deal with a theme continuously throughout history instead of with the stratum of a single period. It cuts through the epochs which compose other books in the series and discusses occasionally the same materials in a different context. It is our hope that by treating a variety of epochs, areas, individual planners, and theoretical problems—like fortification—we can employ the expertise of a considerable number of authors to develop a fairly comprehensive history of urbanism.

G. R. C.

INTRODUCTION

Man's desire and need for protection are as old as his aggressive impulses, and few of his occupations have absorbed as much of his attention, time, effort, and capital as the design and construction of defenses against the transgressions of his human enemies. Since neolithic times he has endeavored to render his settlements safe from aggression by surrounding them with massive defensive structures that have become enduring records of his material progress on the one hand, and impressive monuments to his bellicose inclinations on the other. And if the combination of the explosive shell with the rifled gun-barrel in the nineteenth century finally rendered fixed circumvallations* obsolete, the persistence of earmarking large percentages of national budgets for "defense" suggests that man's age-old fears have remained the same and that his technological progress has not been matched in the field of human relations.

It may be assumed that even paleolithic cave dwellers protected the entrances to their caverns in some form against unwelcome incursions of either wild animals or hostile visitors. But only during the neolithic period, with the shift from a hunting and food-gathering economy to an agricultural one, and man's change from a nomadic to a settled way of life, do his defensive structures take on the monumental forms of permanent fortifications. Since that time he has surrounded most of his larger settlements with fixed lines of prepared defenses, in the hope that they might either discourage aggression or permit the settlers to repel attacks successfully.

Until about 1500, for some nine millennia, urban defenses generally consisted of a high girdle wall reinforced with towers and fronted by a deep, wide ditch. Wall design, tower arrangement, and the protection of gates were subject to frequent modifications, as their builders tried to cope with improving siege methods and the ever-increasing power of weapons. But even after the sixteenth century, when the design of fortifications underwent its most radical change under the impact of newly developed firearms, the basic concept—of surrounding an inhabited area with a continous line of permanent defenses—remained the same. The primary purpose of these urban enclosures, of course, was to protect the cities they surrounded. But they also had numerous side effects, both good and bad, upon the growth and life of their wards. Every fortified city bore the stamp of its defenses and even today, with most of the former fortifications either built over or razed, cities that had once been

* Consult Glossary, pp. 119–120, for technical terms used throughout the text.

fortified retain much of the character that had been shaped by their enceintes.

Perhaps the most important among the positive effects of an enceinte was its function of effectively controlling urban sprawl. Walls established definite limits for a civic organism; they set it off emphatically from the surrounding countryside and firmly enclosed all major civic activities within their boundaries. Renaissance humanists liked to compare them to the skin of the human body that held the inner organs in place. Walls framed and monumentalized the urban fabric; they made it a dominant focal point of the landscape and gave it the stamp of individuality. Few walled cities looked alike, and citizens could identify with their home towns to a degree that modern man, mobile again and accustomed to standardized and relatively featureless urban pictures, will find difficult to appreciate. Well-designed and constructed walls were objects of civic pride and regarded as prime indicators of a city's wealth and power. The universal importance attached to them in the past is amply reflected in hundreds of ancient and medieval pictorial representations in which towered ring walls were used as standard symbols for "city."

Not all the effects of an enceinte upon the urban body were favorable, however, and the humanistic simile of the human skin is only partly true. While circumvallation was a limiting factor in the good sense mentioned above, it also could become a burdensome constricting agent. It often retarded and sometimes severely hampered a city's development. The degree to which a city's plan and appearance were affected by an enceinte, for better or for worse, varied with its site, the state of weaponry at its age, the purpose of the city's foundation, and the amount of *a priori* planning that preceded its development. Among these, the choice of a site was probably the most significant single factor that shaped a city's growth pattern and urban picture. Traditionally the demands to be met included a healthy climate; a year-round fresh-water supply; a fertile surrounding countryside; accessibility to trade routes; safety from floods, avalanches, and landslides; and safety from enemies. The last consideration, although not always decisive, generally was of primary importance to city founders.

Mountain plateaus, hilltops, and peninsulas were usually regarded as most easily defensible. Foundations on open plains meant either that the founders had confidence in their ability to defend the city under adverse conditions, or that considerations other than safety were more important to them. Once chosen, the site would impose itself upon the city in varying degrees. On a hilltop, for instance, the area was usually restricted and the city's propensity for growth limited; regular street plans were rarely possible or practicable, and building density tended to be high. On a flat and open plain, on the other hand, growth was limited primarily by traffic and economic considerations; regular street plans were both possible and frequent, but the problem of defense became more complex and its solution more expensive.

Within the limitations dictated by its site, a city could develop in one of two basic fashions: it could be built up according to a predetermined plan, or it could be permitted to grow naturally by agglomeration into an unplanned city. Fortifications might be added to the urban body at any stage of its development. Frequently the site was fortified first and the city built later into its prepared defenses. No matter what the sequence, the planning of an enceinte was crucial for the town's subsequent development. If the defensive line was drawn too tightly, the city's potential growth could be severely stunted. If drawn too loosely, defense became more difficult as interior lines of communication were lengthened and more manpower was needed to man the ramparts. Throughout history planners were vexed by this choice and their answer generally had to be a delicate compromise between the needs of the moment and their expectations for the town's future. As might be expected, the decisions made were not always the correct ones. A number of extant fortification lines that were never more than partially filled with habitations testify to the unwarranted optimism of their planners. Palmanova, a Renaissance town planned for 20,000 people, has never attracted more than 5,000 inhabitants to this day. Even more numerous are instances in which enceintes had to be abandoned or razed within decades of their completion to make room for unforeseen urban expansions.

Other knotty problems that constantly faced planners were the manner in which a city's street plan should be adjusted to its fortifications, and the extent to which civilian convenience should be subordinated to military demands. Often the problem was side-stepped, as street plan and defenses were treated as separate and independent elements. But even in unplanned cities that were surrounded by walls which were unrelated to the urban body the number and placement of gates would invariably raise problems. Since city gates were usually considered to be the most vulnerable spots of a defensive system, their number had to be kept at a minimum and their placement carefully planned. Thus, traffic in and out of a town became automatically restricted; the inconvenience to civilians could be, but was not always, alleviated if street plan and fortifications were designed in unison. This type of unified planning, found in colonial foundations of all periods, became the rage during the Renaissance. Although few of them were ever realized, the numerous and elaborate theoretical studies produced during that time represent one of the most fascinating chapters in the history of urbanism.

Finally, any change in weaponry or siege methods had to be countered by corresponding changes in the design of the defenses, if the defenders were to be given any hope of successfully resisting the growing offensive power of potential aggressors. This necessity could lead to a complete razing of outdated fortifications and their replacement, often along new lines, with modern ones. But, since this practice was extremely costly, every effort would first be made to modify extant fortifications and to strengthen them in the hope that they could be made to meet new and increased demands. Occasionally, however, the need for modern defenses would coincide with that for urban expansion and a new fortification ring could be planned and built to serve both purposes.

These introductory comments should suffice to suggest to the reader that the relation of fortification to city planning is a complex subject indeed. The great variety of conditions combined with the numerous possible solutions and the fact that similar problems often, but not always, were solved in a similar manner in different historical periods makes any systematic attempt at typological or chronological classification an encyclopedic enterprise. The present volume, far from claiming to be comprehensive, can only hope to provide the reader with a summary of major planning trends that seem to have dominated in certain Western cultures and periods, and to warn him that for every generalization made, there are bound to be numerous exceptions. And if the emphasis on Italian monuments, particularly for the Renaissance period, seems rather heavy, it reflects not only the author's greater familiarity with the cities of the Appenine peninsula, but also his conviction that it was indeed in Italy where, in the field of fortification at least, the great transformation took place that changed ancient and medieval planning methods to modern ones.

PREHISTORIC ORIGINS

Man's epochal transition from the nomadic ways of a hunter and
food-gatherer to the settled life of a food-producer is now generally
believed to have occurred in the Near East sometime between
10,000 and 7000 B.C. At that time a village-based agricultural economy appears to have developed in the so-called Fertile Crescent, the
foothills of the mountain ranges surrounding the Mesopotamian valley. Moving from cave mouths and temporary hunter's camps into
self-built, permanent habitations, man embarked upon the great ad-
venture of domesticating animals and plants.

The transition was slow and gradual, and, for a long time, hunting remained a major food source and continued to be practiced
side by side with incipient agriculture. But by about 8000 B.C. a
village economy seems to have been fairly well established. These
early settlements were little more than small clusters of mud-brick
huts housing a handful of families who worked the surrounding
fields. But occasionally a village, favored by a location near the
source of valuable raw materials or at the crossing of trade routes,
would attract a larger population in which farmers would mingle
with hunters, traders, and artisans to produce the mixed economy
that forms the basis for the development of an urban culture. As
these early "towns" grew in importance and wealth, their inhabitants evidently felt the need to protect themselves, their interests,
and their possessions against the transgressions from their less-
fortunate and envious neighbors or from nomadic tribes that continued to roam the region. To ward off organized attacks from out-
siders, they surrounded their settlements with walls.[1]

Once man had learned to build permanent shelters strong enough
to protect himself and his family not only from the elements but
also from wild beasts, the thought to surround an entire settlement
with a wall must have been near at hand when the collective security
of a town or village was threatened by man's most cunning enemy,
man himself. No other motivation for the origin of fortification was
really needed. Lewis Mumford may be right in saying that organized
warfare was a product of civilization, but there is no need to accept
his neat, but untenable, hypothesis that fortification began with the
strongholds from which hunters-turned-rulers controlled the farm-
ing population of the surrounding countryside.[2]

Mumford theorizes that, during the slow and gradual transition
from hunting to agriculture, a certain percentage of the population
persisted in its hunting ways and that these hunters, by preserving

their skill in the use of arms, became first the protectors, and eventually the rulers, of the agricultural population.[3] The fortified strongholds of these hunter-rulers began to serve as storage places for booty, arms, and surplus agricultural products; settlers were encouraged to build their houses near these citadels and eventually permitted to protect their settlement with its own walls. Later, when these chiefs took on the functions of priests, their citadels acquired religious significance and became the sites for the cities' major shrines. Thus Mumford ascribes a development to prehistoric settlements that is similar to Armin von Gerkan's description of the rise of Greek towns during the archaic period.[4] However, the finds made at Jericho, which are conveniently bypassed by Mumford, and at Çatal Hüyük, which had not yet been discovered at his writing, effectively deprive his theory of its foundations.

The site of Jericho, near a year-round spring on a plateau overlooking the Jordan river, was inhabited since the ninth millennium B.C.* Around 8000 B.C. the town experienced a spectacular development that saw its population rise to an estimated 2,000 people.[5] Originally the town was not fortified, but its growing, trade-based wealth apparently brought the need for protection that resulted in the earliest-known permanent stone fortifications. By about 7500 B.C. the town was surrounded by a wide rock-cut ditch and a massive stone wall that is preserved to a height of almost four meters. Built into this wall was a round tower, some eight meters in diameter and preserved to a height of over eight meters, with a well-built interior staircase that gave access to its top (*Fig. 1*). Not enough of the town has been excavated to show either its street plan or whether the tower was a single structure, like a medieval keep, or one of several which formed a complete defensive system. There is no evidence that these Jericho fortifications were preceded by a separate stronghold or citadel. The massive scale and construction of the Jericho walls suggests, however, that they were not the first of their kind, but that they may have been preceded by even older town walls at other sites that still await the excavator's pick.

A very different defensive concept was realized about a thousand years later at Çatal Hüyük in Anatolia.[6] A mound covering some 32 acres revealed the multiple layers of a town that flourished from about 6500 to 5650 B.C. On a single site it became possible to trace the early history of man for the better part of a millennium and to follow him through one of the most crucial periods in his past, when he made the transition from a food-gathering to a food-producing economy. The finds reveal that hunting did indeed persist for a long time side by side with agriculture, but there is no evidence to sug-

* A map of key sites mentioned in the text will be found at the beginning of the book.

gest a rise in the hunter's importance and prestige during this transitional period. On the contrary, wall paintings, sculptures, and artifacts reflect a gradual change in the social structure in which the importance of women rose as that of the hunters declined.

A peculiarity of Çatal Hüyük's plan is its complete lack of streets. Single-storied mud-brick houses were built one onto the next without doors and their entrances were through the roof (*Figs. 2–3*). This solid building mass was interrupted only by an occasional open court which did not serve as a traffic agent, however, but as a garbage dump. This building method, which has survived in parts of Anatolia and Iran, was both economical, as several houses shared common walls, and practical in an earthquake-prone region, as the houses braced each other for greater stability. Also, since the blank walls of the houses presented a continuous and unbroken front toward the outside, they formed an effective defensive system that obviated the need of additional walls for the town's protection. An attacker who managed to breach the outside wall at any point would find himself not inside the town but inside a single room, with the defenders waiting for him on the roof.

It may be argued that Çatal Hüyük's defenses were not a planned system of fortification as were Jericho's, but rather the accidental by-product of the people's building methods. If so, the advantages of the method were soon recognized and systematically exploited at Hacilar II, a slightly younger town some 200 miles west of Çatal Hüyük.[7] Although reinforced with sturdy timbers, the mud-brick walls of Çatal Hüyük were relatively thin and probably broken down fairly easily. This defect was remedied at Hacilar, where the town's outside walls were greatly strengthened to increase their resistance to attack (*Fig. 4*). The result was a unique fusion of the urban fabric with its defenses, as one was inseparable from the other.

The Hacilar system of fortification was both logical and extremely efficient for a town in which all traffic moved across rooftops. It was not practical, however, for cities with streets where access to the walls was from the ground and where houses built against these walls became a hindrance to the defenders. Thus, the Anatolian system of defense, like its streetless town plan, had few descendants and the less cohesive system of Jericho, in which a freestanding girdle wall surrounds the inhabited area, became the basis for most later solutions.

PRE-CLASSICAL ANTIQUITY

The flowering neolithic culture of Anatolia faded around 5000 B.C., and the cultural emphasis shifted eastward. The "incipient essays in urban living" of Jericho and Çatal Hüyük became a full-fledged urban culture in Mesopotamia, its development accelerated by the unsettled conditions that prevailed in the region. Frequent dynastic changes, wars, and invasions created a turbulent political and social atmosphere that was conducive for people to cluster together in large, strongly fortified settlements. From the third millennium onward, ramparts become one of the most characteristic features of Mesopotamian urban architecture.

In Mesopotamia the choice of a site from the military point of view was relatively unimportant, as most of the cities were built on flat ground. In the hilly regions around the valley elevated sites might be selected, but in the valley proper only the course of a river or canal could be used strategically and the cities had to rely almost entirely upon their ramparts for safety. Thus, need and urgency combined to stimulate the development of a system of fortification that became a standard in the Western world for several thousand years and was subjected only to relatively minor modifications in later periods.

The great importance which Mesopotamians attached to the walls of their cities is reflected in the long and propitious names they gave to them and the fact that they were placed under the protection of deities.[8] They were the pride of the inhabitants, and it became one of the king's major duties to keep a city's walls in good repair— and to tear down those of his conquered enemies. Size and arrangement of ramparts proclaimed the might and importance of a city, and gateways were designed not only to ward off enemies, but also to impress visitors with the city's wealth.

The main purpose of walls, of course, was to keep enemies from entering a city. To fulfill this function efficiently, they had to be strong enough to resist the battering ram and high enough to prevent escalade; they had to protect the defenders from missiles aimed at them from below and, at the same time, permit them to defend the base of the walls. All of these problems were solved by Mesopotamian builders, sometimes on an awe-inspiring scale. The walls of ancient Ur are reputed to have had a thickness that varied between 25 and 34 meters; and those of Babylon are said to have been 25 meters high and that their towers surmounted them by an additional 5 meters.[9] Crenellations protected the defenders, and galleries projecting from walltops enabled them to defend the base of the walls. For the lateral defense of curtains, towers that projected from the walls were built at arrow-shot's intervals; and to make the approach to the wall as difficult as possible, attackers were forced to cross a wide water-filled ditch. Some of the larger cities surrounded themselves with double, occasionally even triple, wall circuits. Although siege methods also kept improving constantly, the effectiveness of well-designed and well-built fortifications was such that often only long and protracted blockades could force a starving city into surrender.

The shapes of the enceintes were usually square or rectangular, although ovaloid enclosures are found at Ur and Uruk in southern Mesopotamia, and round ones at Zincirli in northern Syria and at some later Parthian and Sassanian foundations. Zincirli (*Fig. 5*) dates either from the late second or early first millennium B.C.[10] It was built on level ground although nearby hills might have been better suited for defense. Forming an almost-perfect circle, the double ring of outer walls is reinforced with 100 towers. Additional walls surround an ovaloid inner town, or citadel, that contained a palace and a temple. No trace of houses has been found in the outer city, indicating that the ambitious plan may never have been completed.

The presence of citadels in many Mesopotamian cities, located either near the town's center or straddling the circumvallation, suggests that they may represent original settlements that were outgrown by their populations. When the citadel became too small for them, people moved to the outside to start a new settlement which, eventually, was fortified with its own walls. The result was an urban type that has been called "citadel city" and has proved to be extremely tenacious. Although with a different genesis, the type appears in archaic Greece and in the Middle Ages, and has survived to our day, as for instance in the Kremlin of Moscow.

Citadel cities could be either the product of a natural development, as described, or they could be planned, as was the case in some Assyrian foundations. These new cities of Assyria were designed after the layout of military camps and are the first representatives of cities that were planned primarily for military purposes, a long-lived strain that was to enjoy particular favor during the Roman period. The type is characterized by extremely regular street layouts that reflect the order and discipline of military ceremonial and battle array. As Oppenheim observes, such orderly arrangements are natural in encampments where the allotment of campsites has to be both equitable and according to rank and status.

Khorsabad (Dur-Sharrukin) seems to have been of this regular type, although nothing of its street plan has survived (*Fig. 6*). The city was built under Sargon II as his residential town and was dedicated in 706 B.C. shortly before the King's death. Only the most important buildings had been finished when it was deserted under his successor.[11] The royal citadel, with its palace and temple, straddles the town's northwest wall. Separately fortified and raised high above the plain on a platform the height of the town wall, it emphatically symbolizes the King's absolute power. Its off-center location corresponds roughly to the placement of the royal tent in Assyrian military camps; according to pictorial representations, it was usually placed near the stockade at the camp's periphery.[12] Private houses that once stood in the city, and with them the town's street plan, have been completely obliterated during the past two-and-a-half millennia. The almost-square enclosure suggests that the plan could have been regular, although the asymmetrical placement of the city gates seems to speak against such regularity.[13]

While little is known of the street plans of Assyrian towns, the appearance of contemporary fortifications can be reconstructed with fair accuracy from numerous reliefs representing Assyrian sieges of enemy strongholds. They show, in considerable detail, not only the tower-reinforced, crenellated walls, often forming double ramparts, but also the siege methods employed to reduce them. In Figure 7, a fortified hilltown with a turreted wall on an artificial platform is under siege by Assyrian troops led by King Tiglath-pileser III. The arrow-shooting king stands behind an armored battering ram that has done considerable damage to one of the town's towers. On the left, a long assault ladder has been placed against another tower and is being mounted by two fully-armed soldiers in what must have been no mean acrobatic feat. The battle has already been won by the Assyrians, as the defenders can be seen surrendering on the ramparts.

On another relief (*Fig. 8*) the battle is still in full swing. Here Ashurnasirpal II besieges a city built on a plain next to a stream. Its defenses are formidable and consist of a triple enceinte on an artificial platform. Again the King is prominently shown, shooting at the defenders from the cover offered by a large siege tower. This siege tower, two-storied, with a built-in battering ram, and fireproofed with a covering of wet animal skins, has been moved close to the wall to raise the attackers to the level of the defenders, and to serve as an assault platform once the latter have been driven from their wall positions. The battering ram has been put out of commission temporarily, as the defenders have snagged its head in a chain and are pulling it upward to render its blows ineffective. Under a hail of stones from above, two Assyrian soldiers with hooks are trying to pull it back down to its effective angle. Below them and slightly to the left, two workmen are busily tunneling through the outer wall near one of the town's gates, while on the far left two sappers in military garb attack the wall with crowbars.

Almost the entire ancient arsenal of offensive weapons and siege machines is illustrated in these two reliefs. The only weapons to be added, before the invention of firearms, were such hurling devices as the ballista and the catapult. But the basic siege methods—battering, sapping, mining, scaling—are represented in their full range and will remain the same throughout the ages. The only significant change will occur with the advent of firearms in the fifteenth century, when the battering ram is largely replaced by the cannon as the chief breaching weapon. These were the standard attack methods that had to be thwarted by the defenders, and the care with which they planned and built their defenses could spell the life or death of their city.

Now and then favorable geographical and stable political conditions combined to render the fortification of individual cities unnecessary. Such seems to have been the case in ancient Egypt where, as far as is known, cities generally were not fortified.[14] Pictorial evidence suggests that the Egyptians were familiar with fortified towns, at least during the predynastic period.[15] But once the country was unified, the Egyptians apparently relied upon a regional defense provided by powerful fortresses erected at the only two major access routes into the country, the eastern Delta approaches and the upper Nile valley in Nubia. Although purely military installations, these Egyptian border fortresses, nevertheless, deserve our attention, as they introduce, in rudimentary form, two features that will become increasingly important in later fortification: the glacis, an artificial downward slope in front of the walls,[16] and an open lane along the interior base of the walls that was a forerunner of the Roman *pomoerium.*

The Nubian forts, which are the better preserved and investigated, were located either on the banks of the river Nile or on islands. On flat terrain they were generally rectangular in shape and surrounded by a wide, dry ditch with brick-faced scarp and counterscarp. On rocky and irregular ground the walls were closely adjusted to the contours of the terrain. The skill with which Egyptian architects could exploit the natural features of a site is nicely illustrated by the Middle Kingdom island fortress at Askut (*Figs. 9–10*). The walls seem to grow from the live rock of the island, their towerlike projections becoming more numerous and more closely spaced where gradual slopes leading up toward the walls demanded the strongest defenses. Spur walls extend eastward and southward from the core of the fortress and effectively deprive a potential enemy of any ground on which he might establish a base of operations. The fortress proper, with its heavily protected gate, occupies the highest point of the island and contains magazines and garrisons neatly laid out along a straight street that runs down the long axis of the compound. Clearly shown is the rudimentary *pomoerium* along the inside base of the walls, which gave the defenders freedom of movement and unimpeded access to all parts of the walls. In addition, of course, all the defensive features found in Mesopotamia, such as towers, crenellations, and projecting galleries were known to and effectively used by the Egyptian architects.[17] All in all, the installation appears to have been highly efficient and, according to Badawy, was constructed with the same care that the Egyptians devoted to the building of their temples and tombs.

Geographically even more isolated, and thus, perhaps, even more fortunate, was the island of Crete, the focal point of the Aegean Bronze Age culture that flourished to the north of Egypt. No fortresses, citadels, or fortified cities have been found on this island whose rulers seem to have relied upon a powerful fleet to keep potential enemies off its shores. Conditions on the mainland of Greece, however, were far from ideal, and the Mycenaeans, who dominated the last phase of the Aegean age, hoped to find security in strongly fortified citadels. Neither purely military installations, like the Egyptian fortress at Askut, nor cities, these fortified residences of local rulers frequently seem to have served as crystallization points for the development of settlements in their immediate neighborhood. This must have been true particularly of those which were favorably located near navigable rivers, harbors, or the crossings of trade routes. Once a defensible site had been adequately fortified, it assured its occupants not only safety from enemies but also dominance over the surrounding territory. The neighborhood of the castle was likely to attract settlers who hoped to enjoy its protection and to profit from its offers of employment. In short, a development like that proposed by Lewis Mumford for prehistoric settlements may well have occurred here, a development similar to that of early Greek archaic and German medieval towns.

The best-known and best-preserved example of the numerous Mycenean citadels that once dotted Greece is Tiryns (*Fig 11*). Its cyclopean walls, over eight meters thick in many places, rise from the live rock of a small but steep hill and embrace a handful of buildings like an impregnable shell. Despite their irregular course, due to the close adjustment to the hilltop contours, the walls are closely welded to the core buildings and the entire layout suggests unified planning.[18] The heart of the complex, the royal megaron, is carefully screened from the outside world by a baffled approach that leads between massive walls through multiple fortified and ceremonial gates, a tortuous road designed for defensibility rather than easy access. A ramp leads to the outermost gate from the left side in a manner that may have been used first in Mesopotamia and that was to become a near-standard in later fortification designs. Its rationale is based on the fact that an approaching enemy would hold his weapons in his right hand and carry the shield on his left arm, thus exposing his unprotected side to the defenders on the walls.

These Mycenean citadels were permanently inhabited strongholds and, according to Von Gerkan,[19] were not intended to serve as refuges for the population of neighboring towns. Tiryns may have been an exception, as the fortified enclosure adjacent to the upper citadel is best explained as a refuge (*Fluchtburg*) for the people of an unfortified nearby settlement.[20] It is large enough to have accommodated not only a few hundred people, but also sufficient livestock to permit the defenders to withstand a protracted siege. In peacetime this lower citadel, which contained no permanent buildings, may have served to house a garrison in tents or other temporary shelters. Thus, Tiryns may illustrate a method that was frequently employed, both earlier and later, to provide for the safety in wartime of a limited civilian population that lived either in an unwalled town or on scattered farms nearby.

CLASSICAL ANTIQUITY

After the Dorian invasions, the incipient urbanism of the early Greeks appears to have developed in a manner similar to that of the Myceneans. Local rulers established themselves in fortified strongholds, often in reconstructed Mycenean citadels, from which they controlled the surrounding countryside upon which they depended for their food supply. Villages might develop in their neighborhood, frequently also on the sites of earlier settlements. Occasionally neighboring villages would join to form a "polis," but as long as these early towns were ruled by kings or oligarchs they generally were not walled, as the rulers were not particularly interested in furthering the independence of their subjects.

While some city walls may have existed earlier, the circumvallation of Greek towns became general practice only during the sixth century B.C. and seems to have been the product of democracy and the consequent awakening of civic consciousness. Fortification became a symbol of a free and autonomous society of citizens, and separate strongholds were no longer tolerated in their midst. Walls of the old citadels, especially those that separated them from the towns, were razed and only those that fitted into the new urban fortification lines were left intact. Thus in Greece city walls were never an original urban component, but always an addition that was made after the towns had been well developed. Once built, however, they provided the city with a clear and definite boundary that must have remained valid for fairly long periods, as any change would have involved extensive and costly reconstructions.

Archeological evidence for archaic fortifications is extremely scarce, due largely to the destruction wrought by the Persians; it becomes somewhat more ample for the fifth and later centuries. Reconstruction after the Persian wars led to a flowering of urban culture and of city planning both in Greece and in Asia Minor. The rebuilding of Miletus in 479 B.C. produced not only the first example of a fully developed Hippodamian plan but also extensive fortifications that completely enclosed the city (*Fig. 22*). In a manner characteristic of Greek military planning, the original wall circuit extended southward to include a dominant height well beyond the limits of the town proper. When this defensive line was shortened during the Hellenistic period, the new south wall became one of the most sophisticated fortification systems of the ancient world (see pp. 24–26 below).

Typically Greek, also, are the fortifications of Knidos (*Fig. 12*).

The walls on the peninsula are presumed to enclose the site of the destroyed archaic town. A new Knidos was built on the mainland after the Persian wars, perhaps as late as the fourth century B.C. A Hippodamian street plan, placed against the southern slopes of a steep range of hills, is loosely circumscribed by a tower-studded girdle wall that has no relation to the town plan. Town and walls exist side by side in curious incongruity, the gridiron plan expressing contempt for the irregularities of the site, while the walls take full strategic advantage of the terrain's natural contours.

A similar discrepancy appears at Priene (*Fig. 13*). As at Knidos, a Hippodamian plan has been impressed upon a sloping site for which it seems ill suited. Again the organically planned, contour-hugging walls stand in no relation to the abstract town plan, although visually they seem to anchor the town to the cliffs behind it and keep it from sliding down the hill. The lower three-fourths of the town is fairly tightly circumscribed, but on the north side the walls reach out well beyond the city to encompass the mountain top. Here as at Knidos the potential enemy had to be kept from establishing himself on a height from which he might dominate the city. As usual in Greek fortification, the enceinte encloses an area much larger than the city and thus, planned or unplanned, makes some allowance for population growth and additional construction between the town's northern edge and the foot of the cliff. The sawtooth design of the southern and eastern walls, the teeth arranged to menace the unprotected right side of an attacker, obviated the construction of towers by substituting a more economical and moderately effective construction method which, however, suffered from the disadvantage that exterior wall surfaces could be protected from one side only.

Priene was a mid-fourth-century foundation, and the design of its walls, based upon the traditional concept of a passive defense, was already outdated by defensive innovations that were applied and tested in the Greek colonies in Sicily. Until the fourth century, the defenders relied primarily upon the height and strength of their wall to keep an enemy at bay and, while under attack, they seldom left its protection. Siege engines, like the battering ram, had to be brought close to the wall to be effective, and the defenders, from the cover of crenellated wall-tops and towers, would try to neutralize them at close range. But shortly after 400 B.C. fortifications were built at Syracuse and Selinus in Sicily which express a radical change in defensive concepts. Their design suggests that the age-old strategy of passive defense was being replaced by one of active defense in which the beleaguered garrison would leave the protection of its walls in frequent sorties to disrupt the enemy's siege preparations and destroy his weapons.[21]

Syracuse (*Fig. 14*) was a Corinthian colony, founded in 734 B.C., which grew to become one of the richest and most powerful cities of the ancient world, a rival of Athens, Rome, and Carthage. The colony soon outgrew Ortygia, the small peninsula on which it was founded, and spread to the mainland where it covered the southern slopes of the large triangular Epipolae plateau. Satellite settlements developed at Neapolis, Tyche, and Achradine, of which only the last was permanently fortified. The most populous districts of Neapolis and Tyche were protected only by temporary earth-works when Syracuse was besieged by the Athenians in 415 B.C. During the long, two-year siege the Athenians occupied the high ground of the plateau and launched their attacks upon the city from above. The defenders were hard pressed and only the indecisiveness of Nicias, the Athenian commander, seems to have saved the city.

The painful and near-disastrous experience of the Athenian siege was well remembered by Dionysius the Elder who ruled Syracuse from 405 to 367 B.C. To deny future aggressors the advantage of high ground, Dionysius decided to fortify the entire Epipolae plateau, and, between 402 and 397, the Syracusans, in a stupendous effort, constructed close to 20 kilometers of wall along the upper edges of the plateau. At the plateau's western end, which is also its highest point, these walls were anchored by one of the most powerful fortresses of antiquity. By 396 B.C. these defenses, although not completed, were in good enough condition to withstand, successfully, one of the numerous Carthaginian sieges to which Syracuse was exposed (others were defeated in 480, 343, and 310 B.C.).

The key to the Dionysian defenses was the Castel Euryelos (*Figs. 15–17*).[22] Situated on a rocky ledge some 60 meters wide, the fortress flanks the main gateway to the plateau. The gate (*Fig. 15,* K) itself is strongly protected by projecting walls that are angled like a Baroque tenaille, and by short wall sections that create a baffled approach. But the gate's main protection is the fortress on its southern flank. It consists of two spacious enclosures of which the smaller (G) is fronted by a group of five massive towers (*Fig. 15,* F).[23] The fort's western approach is protected by three deep, rock-cut ditches of which the outermost is about 200 meters distant from the five-towered keep. Enclosed by the reverse angles of the second and third ditches is a wall-protected terrace (C) that resembles a modern ravelin. The innermost ditch (D), its mouth sealed with a sturdy wall (*Fig. 15,* M) (shown in the foreground of *Fig. 16*) opens onto the plain, enabling the defenders to pour forth to attack from the back any enemy who might offend the gateway. All outworks behind the second ditch are honeycombed with a complex system of subterranean corridors and galleries (*Fig. 15,* items 2, 3, 4, 5; their combined length totals about 480 meters) that permitted a rapid shifting of forces to any part of the fortification system. Although they formed part of the fortress, these outworks could function independently; in fact, the third ditch (*Fig. 15,* D) and the platform in front of it must have been the main center of defensive action. It is estimated that up to a thousand men could have been held in readiness inside the third ditch, to be channeled to any threatened part of the fortifications through underground passages; they could be shifted rapidly either to the platform to fight off a frontal attack, or out into the plain, or, through a long subterranean corridor, to the gateway to reinforce its garrison. The new concept of active defense is fully expressed not only in the extensive underground network of communications, but also in the relatively light construction of the fort's walls which average only two to three meters in thickness. In short, elasticity and mobility have replaced the old principle of defense by inert mass.

The same new approach to defensive tactics is expressed by the fortifications of the north gate of Selinus (*Figs. 18, 19, 20, 21*). A seventh-century Greek colony, the town was destroyed after a Carthaginian siege in 409 B.C. It was rebuilt and refortified after it regained its independence in 397 B.C.[24] The densely built-up, pear-shaped plateau is encircled by a girdle wall, all parts of which are easily accessible from the interior along a wide, extremely well-developed *pomoerium.* The overall aspect of the town's plan, with its emphatic crossing of north–south and east–west axes, its tight circumvallation and wide *pomoerium*, is peculiarly un-Greek and, except for the irregular trace of the walls, seems to forecast Roman planning methods.

The *pomoerium* is interrupted on the short north side of the town where buildings nestle against the wall. It may have been deemed unnecessary in this area, since the heavy walls here merely represent the innermost line of defense of a complex and far-flung system of outer fortifications. The design of these outworks reputedly was inspired by Dionysius of Syracuse, and it expresses even more clearly than the Castel Euryelos the new concept of aggressive defense. Behind a deep, wide ditch, two huge, half-round towers are placed at the ends of galleries that form a right angle. The long east–west gallery (its remains are shown in *Fig. 20*) is pierced by numerous small gates or posterns that open directly into the ditch and give the structure a curiously porous appearance, very different from the hermetically sealed aspect of earlier walls. This gallery was designed to permit the defenders to shift in and out of their fixed defenses as the occasion demanded, and to make their sorties under the covering fire from multiple embrasures in walls and flanking towers.

Some two hundred years later what had been tried along a front of some 50 meters at Selinus was applied on a much larger scale at Miletus (*Figs. 22, 23, 24*).[25] Sometime, early in the second century B.C. (between 200 and 190 B.C., according to Von Gerkan) the long southern loop of fifth-century walls that enclosed the Kalabaktepe hill was replaced by a new south wall which shortened the original defensive line from 1,800 to 500 meters. Although this realignment placed the new wall in a strategically weak position, as the open plain in front of it was large enough to allow an enemy full poliorcetic development, the disadvantage was offset by a first-class defensive system that illustrates the Hellenistic art of fortification at its very best.

An essentially straight line was dissolved into 8 lightly slanted curtains resembling the serrated southern wall of Priene. Here, however, each curtain is anchored by a powerful tower that protects a small gate as well as adjacent wall sections. Strong projection from the walls puts neighboring towers in full view of each other and enables them to cover the curtain between them from both sides.[26] The spacing of the towers at an average interval of 60 meters, almost double the effective range of ancient bows and arrows, indicates that the defense relied heavily upon mechanically operated weapons. In fact, the large embrasures in the towers, especially those of their upper levels (see *Fig. 24*), must have been designed for such engines as the ballista. To protect the numerous wall openings, the entire wall system must have had extensive outworks, although little evidence for such has been found so far. The overall design of this south wall suggests great flexibility and plans for an extremely active defense based upon frequent sorties by the garrison to keep the enemy away from the walls and to disrupt his siege preparations.

The key to the defensive system was the "Holy Gate" (shown on the far right in *Fig. 23*). In a manner typical of Greek classical fortification, the original gate had been aligned with the fifth-century walls and showed no concern whatever for the city's street plan. When a new gate was fitted to the Hellenistic walls, the old gate was left standing to create a fortresslike, triangular enclosure that may have served for the stationing of reserves in wartime; from here raiding parties that had sallied forth from one of the posterns could be quickly reinforced. In fact, through the nine wall openings in this south front, the defenders could have poured an entire army into the field within minutes to challenge the enemy in open battle. The tentative solutions of Syracuse and Selinus found full fruition and large-scale application at Miletus in a highly flexible defensive system that stresses mobility and aggressiveness and represents the high-water mark of ancient urban fortification. Neither the Etruscans nor the Romans produced anything as subtle and sophisticated as these Hellenistic Miletan defenses.

The Etruscans relied primarily upon easily defensible sites for the safety of their cities. In their search for naturally strong sites they were favored by the geological formation of their heartland. In southern Tuscany and northern Lazio the gently rolling landscape is crisscrossed by riverbeds that have cut deeply into the soft tufa soil, leaving mesalike plateaus with steep, clifflike walls (*Fig. 27*). These plateaus, along with occasional hilltops, became the preferred sites for Etruscan town foundations; only now and then would a colonial foundation (Marzabotto) or a harbor (Spina) be built on flat ground.

In contrast to general Greek practice, Etruscan towns were walled from the very beginning. Once a strong site had been chosen, the next consideration was its fortification. Walls, constructed in large blocks of either tufa or local stone (*Fig. 26*), closely followed the contours of the terrain; they were not always continuous, but served mainly to strengthen the natural features of the site in such a way that all accesses to the plateau were protected, either naturally or artificially. The result was meandering, extremely irregular wall circuits that often enclosed areas much larger than the ones that were eventually built up (*Fig. 25*).[27]

Little is known of Etruscan street plans, as few towns have been excavated. Many of the sites were so well chosen that they have been inhabited ever since their foundation, and such Etruscan centers as Perugia, Volterra, Tarquinia, Orvieto, and others have remained bustling communities to this day. It may even be assumed that their general appearance, although most of their present components are medieval, has not changed too much since Etruscan times. Orte (*Fig. 28*), as seen from the distance, probably looks today pretty much the way it did some 2,500 years ago. A dense cluster of habitations seems to grow out of the tufa of a small plateau with sides so steep that little additional fortification was needed to render the town unassailable.

If any inference can be drawn from Etruscan necropoli, irregular street plans may have been the rule in Etruscan towns, although regular plans have been found occasionally in colonial and harbor foundations. On irregular sites the street plans probably were adjusted to the demands of the terrain. Whether this practice resulted in any sort of integration between city plan and walls remains doubtful; the two elements probably existed side by side as they did in Greek cities. Thus, diametrically opposed planning and growth processes produced similar results. In one case, the town was built first and then surrounded with walls; in the other, the walls were constructed first and the city was built into them. In neither case were the two urban components planned in unison and, as a consequence, the city and its walls were independent of each other and functioned separately.

The Romans made few, if any, novel contributions to city planning. In the design of fortifications they seemingly ignored the sophisticated solutions of Hellenistic designers and returned to the earlier standard of hermetically sealed enclosures, confining their efforts to the improvement of such details as towers, galleries, and crenellations. And even in the field of weaponry they made no new inventions, which seems surprising in view of the dominant role which the military establishment played in Roman affairs. Any lack of originality, however, was amply compensated for by an unparalleled organizational skill, a willingness to adopt new and foreign ideas and the ability to develop them to their logical conclusions. Unified urban planning, in which the city and its defenses were treated as a single conception, had been tried occasionally in earlier times, notably by the Assyrians, but never before, and rarely afterward, was it applied with such systematic consistency as it was by the Romans.

Departing from Etruscan and Greek concepts, Roman urbanism developed an Italian colonial style which provided the basis for the standard plan of later colonial foundations in the conquered provinces. The original purpose of Roman colonies was the purely military one of establishing strong points in hostile country and, while this limited scope eventually was expanded to incorporate cultural and propagandistic elements, these foundations never lost their military character. The primacy of military considerations in Roman city planning is clearly expressed in the foundation ceremonies which the Romans reputedly adopted from the Etruscans. Of the ritual's four successive steps the first is partly, the second entirely, motivated by military requirements. The first rite, the *inauguratio*, determined the future town's location; supposedly based on auguries, the choice in early foundations generally fell on easily defensible sites. The second rite, the *limitatio*, determined the town's circumference; the chosen area was circumscribed with a plowed furrow; the plowed earth was thrown inward and symbolized the wall, while the furrow itself represented the edge of the ditch; at the sites of future gates the plow was lifted (*portare*: to carry; *porta*:

gate). The last two rites were the *orientatio*, in which the street net was laid out and oriented; and the *consecratio*, in which the town was placed under the protection of its patron deity.[28]

All of these rites may well have been performed at the foundation of Cosa (*Figs. 29, 30*), the first Roman outpost to be established in Etruscan territory in 273 B.C. and a fairly typical representative of an early Italian colony.[29] A medium-sized town, planned for some ten to twelve thousand settlers, Cosa was carefully sited on top of a fairly steep coastal hill some 150 kilometers north of Rome. A lagoon at the hill's eastern foot was converted into the city's port.

The town's wall closely circumscribes the crest of the hill, taking full advantage of cliffs and rocky outcroppings. Along those stretches where the wall is easily approachable, it is reinforced with strongly projecting towers whose average interval of 30 meters corresponds to the range of ancient archers. Stone for the wall was quarried from the north side of the hill in such a way that the quarry formed a rough ditch that protected the towerless north wall. The blocks of stone, averaging one ton in weight, were assembled to form a dry-jointed polygonal wall of the revetment type which is higher on the outside than the inside. The slightly battered exterior face was carefully smoothed to impede escalade. No traces of wall walks or of battlements have been found, but it may be assumed that some kind of breastworks, probably constructed in coursed rubble work, originally crowned walls and towers. While polygonal town walls are typical of early Roman colonies in central Italy (Cora, Norba, Alatri), most of them are towerless. The two towered fronts at Cosa are an innovation that may reflect the influence of Hellenistic military engineering; they probably represent the first, still tentative, application of knowledge gathered by the Romans during the Samnite and Pyrrhic campaigns in southern Italy.[30]

The Cosa walls, neatly flanked by a well-developed *pomoerium*, are pierced by four openings—three gates and a postern. The gateways are of the "interior court" or "propylon" type, with the gatehouse projecting inward from the wall. They anchor a slightly irregular street plan of the gridiron type that has been angled to cut across the sloping terrain at the minimum average grade. Archaic, compared with later Roman plans, are the rather long and narrow block shapes of varying proportions, and the fact that no single street cuts across the town from gate to gate. Instead, the gates are so disposed as to provide the forum with the shortest possible access routes, thus stressing its administrative function and, indirectly, expressing the town's basic purpose as the region's military and administrative center. The importance of civil and military magistrates was foremost, and the streets are treated as access channels to the seat of their authority. One of the central ideas of Roman urbanism is here expressed in its germinal stage; it will experience monumental development in later, more regularly planned colonial foundations.

In its overall aspect the Cosa plan differs strikingly from those of Greek cities. Town and enceinte have been planned in a single cast; the two parts belong together and are inseparable; they function in unison and thus express the essentially military character of the foundation. If the plan falls short of the regularity expected in a military installation, it is due mainly to the irregularities of the site. Later colonial foundations, generally built on flat ground, will permit Roman planners to develop not only regular, but symmetrical, plans that become concrete embodiments of military order and discipline.

It has been said that love of symmetry in art is a quality typical of civilizations that are ruled by a strong central authority, and Egypt, Assyria, and Persia are often cited as examples of this trend. Under the Romans symmetry seemingly became a ruling formal principle for the entire civilized world; and nowhere does it find fuller expression than in the colonial foundations of the imperial period. And if the above generalization is suspect, then the rigid symmetry of the Roman "castrum" plan can find ample justification in its military nature.[31] For these imperial colonies, like their republican predecessors, were first and foremost Roman military outposts. When they were endowed with the additional function of serving as cultural fountainheads for the romanization of conquered territories, they may have blossomed into monumental showpieces designed to impress the barbarians with the might and universality of Roman power, but they always retained their military character and express to perfection the disciplined order and uniformity so essential to military establishments.

An almost ideal version of the castrum plan is that of Timgad in North Africa (Fig. 31). Founded by Trajan in 100 A.D. and built by his soldiers, the town was destroyed by natives in the sixth century; it was partially rebuilt by the Byzantines in the seventh century, to be destroyed again by the Arabs. The division of the master square into square units and subunits achieves a close and orderly integration of the street plan with its circumvallation and, symbolically, seems to reflect the static organization of a military hierarchy.[32] The forum, seat of temporal authority, is prominently located near the town's center and is approached, but not crossed, by the main streets. The plan is orderly, compact, practical, and efficient, and all elements of the urban body are firmly contained and kept in their proper places by the close-fitting wall enclosure. While this tight, rectilinear enceinte acts as an effective frame for the civic body, it has the disadvantage of hindering urban growth and expansion. The Roman system, thus, is less flexible than that of the Greeks. If a Roman city grew beyond its prescribed boundaries, an irregular belt of constructions sprang up outside the wall which, in antiquity, was seldom refortified and became a severe impediment to the effectiveness of the original fortifications.

Little is left of the Timgad walls. They may not have looked too different from those of the palace of Diocletian at Spalato which was built some 200 years later (*Fig. 32*). Tower-studded, rectilinear walls with strongly fortified gates surround a *castrum* plan as at Timgad, but may appear more dominant here because the area enclosed is much smaller than that of the north African town. Regardless of possible inaccuracies in the rendering of details, the reconstructed model adequately illustrates the general character of Roman fortifications at the height of their development. Lacking the strategic subtleties of Hellenistic defenses, the Roman system takes advantage neither of staggered wall segments for better flanking, nor of multiple posterns for effective sorties. Even tangentially laid out gate-approaches, that had been used ever since Mycenean times, are ignored. Fortifications have again become primarily breastworks for the defenders who have withdrawn into an impenetrable shell of walls and towers designed for a passive defense.

An explanation for this apparent retrogression in the art of fortification may be found in the general military strategy of the Romans and in the political conditions during the height of their power. After the defeat of the Carthaginians and the conquest of the Hellenistic kingdoms, few of Rome's remaining enemies had either the means or the ability to mount massive, methodical siege operations. Against poorly conceived and ill-prepared sieges, however, solidly constructed fortifications and well-provisioned garrisons could resist almost indefinitely. Since the Romans relied primarily upon their mobile field armies for the defense of the Empire, fortification to them simply became a matter of providing a town's population and its garrison with the means to resist attack until they could be relieved from the outside. Although the Romans did build a fixed regional defensive line, the *limes*, along their northern frontier, the key to their military strategy was the mobility of their legions which could be moved fast and efficiently to threatened areas along a masterfully conceived strategic network of roads. Thus, the task of Roman garrisons was really much simpler than that of their Greek counterparts. A beleaguered Greek city, usually the nucleus of a small, independent state, seldom had hope of getting help from the outside; its garrison generally had to rely upon its own devices and try to break the siege from the inside. The Romans, on the other hand, simply had to hold out until relief arrived.

Roman confidence in the ability of the field armies to keep an enemy out of Italy is amply reflected in the fact that, for almost five hundred years, the cities of the homeland were not even fortified. Only late in the third century A.D., when increasing Germanic pressure threatened to collapse the Empire's northern boundaries, did the Romans decide to fortify their own capital. The Aurelian wall, built between 270 and 282 A.D., was drawn along an irregular trace to surround an already diffused urban fabric that housed close to one million inhabitants. Some 19 kilometers long, pierced by 18 strongly protected gates (*Fig. 33*) and strengthened, at about 30-meter intervals, with 381 square towers (*Fig. 34*), the wall was repeatedly restored and modified and its present appearance is due largely to major reconstructions carried out under Honorius and Arcadius in the early fifth century A.D.[33]

The Aurelian wall was constructed under what its architects must have felt were extremely adverse conditions. All their predispositions for order and symmetry had to be abandoned as they were forced to build an enceinte around a sprawling, shapeless civic body with which it could not be adequately integrated. Furthermore, the wall's meandering course had to be led across relatively bland terrain with few features that lent themselves to strategic exploitation. Under the circumstances, it seems, some of the Hellenistic defensive principles might well have been utilized to advantage in the wall's design, especially since it must have been foreseen that any siege of the Roman capital itself presupposed the defeat of the legions in the field, and that, consequently, there would be little hope that the city could be relieved from the outside. The fact that the Aurelian wall became an hermetically sealed enclosure that differs little in either concept or appearance from the traditional standard of Roman fortification reflects a certain doctrinaire rigidity in the attitude of its planners, a lack of flexibility in the face of changing conditions that constitutes one of the omens for the eventual collapse of the Empire.

The Aurelian wall has served Rome, not always successfully, until 1870, when it was breached for the last time by the modern artillery of the Kingdom of Italy. Still in fair condition, it is the most monumental, although hardly the most inspired, example of late classical fortification that has come down to us and represents that stage of ancient military architecture that was to be perpetuated during the Middle Ages.

THE MIDDLE AGES

During the early Middle Ages the Latin urban culture was temporarily eclipsed by the pastoral culture of the Germanic tribes who swept out of the north to overrun the tottering West Roman Empire. The Mediterranean urban sense, however, never died out completely, and ancient cities, time and again, would rise from conquest and destruction to live on under new rulers. In Italy almost all major medieval towns had existed in antiquity, and in the former Roman provinces many of the old colonial foundations survived into modern times.[34]

The basic unit of Germanic settlement was the individual farm, and the tribes which swept into the Mediterranean basin were ill prepared to perpetuate an urban civilization that was alien to them. Nevertheless, most of the invaders greatly admired Roman culture and their destruction of it was almost inadvertent as they were pressed westward by the Huns who had erupted from the east. Frequently the migrating tribes, once they thought they had found a place to settle, would try deliberately to revive Roman culture which they somehow recognized as superior to their own. By way of consolidating their conquests, they rebuilt and refortified many of the cities they had destroyed, and Gothic, Langobard, and Frankish kings felt themselves to be the heirs and successors of the Roman emperors. Theodoric made Ravenna, the last capital of the West Roman Empire, his residential city; the Langobard kings chose Verona as theirs. And if the efforts of these earlier Germanic kings to extend the life of Rome have gone largely unnoticed, it is due in part to the fact that they are historically overshadowed by the even more concerted and single-minded efforts of Charlemagne who wanted not only to re-establish the glory of ancient Rome, but to uproot Mediterranean culture from its native habitat and export it into northern Europe.

During the early centuries after the fall of the West Roman Empire, invading tribes were seldom able to gain a permanent foothold anywhere, as they would be pushed on by other tribes pressing in behind them. Frequent changes of local rulers and the complete lack of a central governing authority created an atmosphere of turmoil and insecurity that is perhaps best reflected in the almost incredible proliferation of castles all over Europe. Over 20,000 of them were built in Italy alone; the remains of 72 can still be found in the very limited confines of the Val d'Aosta, a narrow valley, 90 kilometers long, on the southwestern slopes of the Alps.[35] Fractionalized power encouraged individual families to establish themselves in fortified residences from which they could extend their rule over limited territories. Preferred sites were hilltops that could be rendered inaccessible with minimum means and effort. If the slopes were steep enough to prevent the deployment of siege machinery, relatively primitive walls sufficed to make a stronghold practically unassailable. Most early medieval castles consisted of little more than high, strongly built walls surrounding a central tower, or keep, that doubled as living quarters and last refuge.

Like the citadels in antiquity, many medieval castles became focal points for urban growth, as settlers moved to their neighborhoods either to enjoy their protection or to take advantage of the employment opportunities they might offer. In fact, many seeds for medieval urbanism were the same as those of antiquity: market places at trade-route crossings where merchants and artisans might settle; individual farms that joined to form villages; ancient settlements and cities, either deserted to be repopulated, or still inhabited and attracting new immigrants. Other crystallization points were the residences, either permanent or temporary, of kings and dukes which had to provide housing for officials, administrators, artisans, and workers. Added to these must be the seats of church authorities (bishoprics) who became major sponsors of the medieval urban revival. While most of these settlements grew irregularly through natural processes of agglomeration, such special purpose foundations as the French *bastides* (comparable to ancient colonies) frequently were laid out and built according to rigid preplanned gridiron patterns. In short, the great variety of origins and growth patterns of medieval cities make the period one of the most fascinating in the history of urbanism.

The process of urban revival begins, haltingly at first, during the ninth century and gradually accelerates as the turbulent political conditions become more settled and orderly. An important factor in fostering urban development and civil consciousness, were the "Rights" which might be delegated to a settlement by a king or local sovereign for services which the town had rendered him (usually the furnishing of troops, equipment, or provisions for the sovereign's army). Among the Rights that could be awarded were those to hold market and to have a court of justice, along with the rights to self-administration and to fortify the settlement. This last one was particularly dear to townships, as strong walls seemed to be the best guaranty that the other rights could be protected and preserved. Thus walls, as they had been in antiquity, again became the symbols of a free society of citizens. As symbols of higher significance, walls came to be considered as not only beneficial and comforting but beautiful. Objects of civic pride, they defined the *civitas* through which man obtained freedom and was relieved from the dangers existing in the open country. The wall became a symbol of the Good, as it detached the city from the countryside (which was considered neither good nor beautiful in the Middle Ages) and converted it into a region of order and justice.[36]

Technical and theoretical problems of fortification had not changed since antiquity, as no new weapons were introduced into the siege arsenal until the thirteenth century.[37] In fact, defense had become simpler, as few of the medieval sovereigns had the means, economic or military, to mount protracted sieges that could compare with those of Roman armies in scale, severity and methodical efficiency. Against shortlived and haphazard attacks, however, even relatively crude versions of the never entirely forgotten Roman method of fortification could offer adequate resistance. The manner in which Roman military architecture found its way into the Middle Ages is strikingly illustrated by Carcassonne which, thanks to Viollet-le-Duc's devoted studies and restorations, owns one of the best preserved and most impressive extant medieval enceintes.[38]

Carcassonne (*Figs. 35, 36*) originally was a Roman *castellum*. In 436 it fell to the Visigoths, who liked its naturally strong hilltop position and made it the key to their French possessions. Among all the barbarians, the Visigoths were the first to appreciate fully the value of Roman military architecture, and, when they refortified Carcassonne, they closely followed earlier Roman construction. Most of the inner enceinte stands on Roman foundations, and the only major change made was the substitution of semicylindrical towers for the square ones that had been used by the Romans (*Fig. 37*; note square Roman base from which the Visigothic tower rises). As had been Roman practice, the lower halves of the towers were constructed solidly to better resist the battering ram; their upper halves were pierced by large arched openings that served as embrasures for mechanically operated weapons. Thus, neither in appearance nor in function did the new wall differ significantly from its Roman predecessor. It proved its effectiveness during the wars against the Franks and Burgundians, as Carcassonne became the last refuge of the Visigoths in France; it did not fall until 713, and then to the Arabs.

Nothing is known of Carcassonne's history for the next four centuries. Around 1130 it was in the hands of the French who, at that time, repaired the old walls and built the castle. In 1240 the French king, Louis IX, relieved the city from a siege by Catalan and Aragonese troops and decided to make it the bulwark of that southern part of his kingdom. He immediately inaugurated an extensive refortification program which provided the town with an outer enceinte and a huge, round barbican on its western flank. When these works were completed in 1285 under Saint Louis' successor Philip the Bold, Carcassonne's fortifications were the strongest of their time, and throughout the Middle Ages the town was considered to be impregnable.

By the time of Carcassonne's second enceinte, medieval military architecture had introduced some significant changes to the traditional designs handed down from the Romans. Most of the innovations seem to have been imported from the Near East by returning crusaders and may reflect the then-current state of Byzantine fortification. The period saw a proliferation of outworks, especially in the form of barbicans that protected gates. Also, towers were built hollow from the base up to permit defenders to give lateral protection to the curtains from embrasures in the tower's lower levels. Most striking, perhaps, are the projecting machicoulis galleries which came into use at about this time and which are one of the most characteristic elements of later medieval fortification. Until the fourteenth century these galleries were generally of wood (*Fig. 38*). At Carcassonne the upper levels of the walls are pierced for the installation of such galleries which, in effect, provided the defenders with an elevated platform outside the wall proper, from which the base of the wall could be protected more efficiently. Portable and quickly assembled when needed, wooden galleries were both practical and economical, but also relatively fragile and inflammable. From the fourteenth century onward they were generally replaced by permanent, corbel-supported stone galleries which were safer and stronger, but also much costlier (*Figs. 50–58*). That wooden galleries did not fare too well under attack is shown graphically in Viollet-le-Duc's neat and instructive illustrations of medieval siege methods, where they are represented as heavily damaged by hurled missiles (*Fig. 39*) and ablaze (*Fig. 40*). Figure 39 also shows several of the then-new counter-poise catapults, or trebuchets, in action. But, otherwise, the basic attack methods have changed very little since Assyrian times (see *Figs. 7, 8*). Crossbow men behind movable shields have replaced the ancient archers, but the cat which protects workers building an approach ramp to the base of the wall (foreground, *Fig. 39*), the battering ram, and the siege tower (middle ground, *Fig. 39*, and *Fig. 40*) have remained the key assault weapons. And pioneers, or sappers, are still attacking the base of the wall with crowbars (*Fig. 38*) as they had two thousand years before. Drastic changes in the methods of offense and defense will occur only during the sixteenth century, when firearms became a serious menace.

The importance that Saint Louis attached to Carcassonne as the key bulwark of his southern possessions was bound to attract new settlers who could not be accommodated within the walled town. Its hilltop location precluded expansion, except possibly toward the west where the slope is relatively gentle. But the decision to keep and to reinforce the old defensive lines had already been made, and, rather than impede the military effectiveness of his fortress town by having its defenses blocked with suburbs, Louis founded a new city a short distance away on the opposite side of the river Aude. This new Carcassonne, from which the modern city evolved, was laid out in the regular grid pattern that Louis and his son adopted for other bastides built during their reigns. Aigues-Mortes (*Fig. 41*), almost contemporary with Carcassonne, was founded by Louis as a Mediterranean port near the mouth of the Rhône. Despite a slightly irregular enceinte, it is typical of many medieval colonial foundations, not only in France, but also in East Germany and north Italy. They are characterized by dry, rational, and efficient checkerboard plans surrounded by powerful fortifications, a combination that clearly expresses their dominantly military purpose.

That gridiron plans and square or rectangular enceintes are not concomitant is shown by Cittadella (*Fig. 42*) where a perfect grid pattern is circumscribed by an almost circular enceinte. The town was founded by Padua in 1220 to confront Treviso and its recent foundation of Castelfranco (1199), and the medieval fortifications of both towns have survived in excellent condition. Like most medieval colonies, including the French bastides, Cittadella and Castelfranco lost their strategic importance toward the end of the Middle Ages and owe their state of preservation to the facts that they were neither exposed to destructive sieges nor considered important enough in later times, to have their fortifications rebuilt or modernized.

Simliar circumstances, fortunate for the historian, have led to the near-perfect preservation, even without the benefit of major restorations, of one of the most impressive medieval enceintes in Italy, that of Montagnana (*Figs. 43–46*). Of pre-Roman origin, the town has a plan that, despite distortions caused by repeated destructions, seems to refer back to the Roman *castrum* type. In the eleventh century Montagnana was the dominion of the Langobard family that later adopted the name of d'Este. It was conquered, destroyed, and rebuilt by Ezzelino da Romano in 1242, and then successively passed under the rules of Padua, the Carrara, Scala, and Visconti families, before becoming a Venetian possession in 1405. After a few more turbulent years during the Venetian war against the League of Cambrai, in which the town changed hands not less than thirteen times, it sank into the relative oblivion that is responsible for its preservation.[39]

Most of Montagnana's walls date from the 1360's when the Carrara refortified the town against Verona and the Scala family. The enceinte is about 2 kilometers long and consists of high brick walls reinforced with tall towers at about 75 meter intervals. A very wide ditch and well-developed glacis compensate for the lack of machicolations on walls and towers which are crowned only by flat-topped, "guelf" merlons (see the swallow-tail design of "ghibelline" merlons in *Fig. 49*). The defensive strength of the system is further enhanced by the ingenious design of the towers, whose polygonal shape enabled the defenders to protect most of their outside surfaces from adjacent curtains in a manner that seems to anticipate the design of Renaissance bastions by some 150 years. A *pomoerium,* the width of one of the town's streets, kept the interior surfaces of the heavily buttressed walls clear of obstructions and facilitated the arming of the open-backed towers (*Fig. 45*).[40] The town's east and west gates are very heavily fortified, as gates were considered the weak points of medieval enceintes and innumerable precautions were taken to render them safe. The west gate, or Rocca degli Alberi (*Fig. 46*), is approached by a fortified bridge that leads across the ditch to a court designed like a trap. This entrance court is surmounted by the town's only machicolated tower, so that an invader could be attacked from above, as well as from all sides. At Montagnana the gate fortifications doubled as individual strongholds for the ruling families (the Castello di San Zeno at the east gate was built by Ezzelino, the Rocca degli Alberi by the Carrara) who, by virtue of their ability to shut off in- or out-bound traffic, could exercise effective control over the town's population.

Montagnana never grew beyond its medieval boundaries, and its walls have kept the civic body intact for over six centuries. Other medieval cities, economically and politically more favored perhaps, were constantly faced with expansion problems, and their growing pains are deeply etched into their urban fabric. The plan of Florence (*Fig. 47*), although less confused than those of many other cities, clearly tells its story of medieval urban sprawl. Originally an Etruscan foundation, Florence became Roman in the second century B.C.; it was destroyed by the Goths, but soon revived and, by 1000 A.D., was again an important community. Suburbs developed outside the Roman walls and when an extension southward of the walls failed to contain them, the entire town was girdled with a new wall in about 1175 A.D. But the town continued to grow outside this new enceinte, and, in 1284, a third wall was begun to enclose the new suburbs.

The regular *castrum* core of Florence is still easily recognizable. Usually the growth of suburbs outside a city's gates was uncontrolled and took place without regard for the plan of the old city. Suburbs generally developed along the traffic arteries which, once they left the gates, veered in the direction of neighboring cities. Since antiquity, these growth patterns have not changed materially to this day. As long as walls represented a city's major defense, however, unplanned urban growth always confronted military planners with the knotty problem of where to build the new defenses. The second and third enceintes of Florence illustrate two possible answers. The second wall was evidently drawn rather tightly around the built-up areas along the shortest practical course. This was the short-range, economical way of solving the problem; it gave protection to the people who clamored for it at minimum cost to the city. Perhaps, to do justice to the planners, no further growth was anticipated, but the town continued to grow, at first implosively, as new settlers naturally wanted to move inside the walls to benefit from the protection they offered. Building density became extremely high, to the point where even the main bridge across the Arno, the Ponte Vecchio, was covered with shops and habitations. When the area inside the walls was saturated with construction, new suburbs developed outside the walls once more and, by 1284, a third enceinte became mandatory. When the decision to build a third enceinte could no longer be circumvented, its planners decided not to repeat the mistake of their predecessors. The new wall was drawn well outside the built-up areas and enclosed large tracts of open country; it was spacious enough to contain the city until the nineteenth century.

The foresight of the thirteenth-century planners, while laudable, may well have been deplored two centuries later when, under the threat of newly developed firearms, their wall became hopelessly outmoded. The very spaciousness of the old enclosure must have voided the pretexts of those who might have wished to advocate the construction of still another, more modern enceinte. Instead, the old walls were reinforced with bastions and with two powerful fortresses, north and south, in what must have seemed like a stop-gap measure to many.

THE MODERN ERA

The fifteenth century is marked by the ascendency of firearms, a new class of weapons that was destined to revolutionize military tactics and render obsolete most past approaches to fortification. Medieval military architecture had been refined to the point where it could offer successful resistance to all known offensive weapons. Stone missiles hurled by catapults could damage, but not break down, well-built walls and the battering ram remained the most effective breaching weapon in a siege train's arsenal. Its use, however, had become extremely hazardous since the advent of machicoulis galleries which had greatly increased the defenders' ability to protect the base of the wall where the battering ram had to be employed. Once more, in the fluctuating contest between defense and offense, the former had been able to neutralize the aggressor's improved siege methods and weapons, and a military impasse often could be resolved only by starving a stronghold into surrender with a long and costly blockade.

Whatever advantage the defenders might have held at the end of the Middle Ages, however, evaporated during the fifteenth century. The cannon provided the attacker with a breaching weapon that rendered the machicoulis galleries useless, as it could do the battering ram's job from a distance that was well beyond the range of traditional weapons. The cannon was an invention of the early fourteenth century, and its emergence as an irresistible siege weapon was, of course, gradual.[41] In the early stages of its development it did not greatly exceed older hurling mechanisms in power or efficiency, since it shot stone balls which tended to shatter upon impact. Only toward the end of the fifteenth century, when iron cannonballs came into general use, did it become the devastating weapon that rendered traditional fortification methods obsolete. Thus, throughout most of the fifteenth century, the defenders had the opportunity to assess its effects and to adjust their defenses accordingly.

Since cannon could also be used by the defenders, early efforts of military engineers were directed toward modifying their structures to permit an efficient deployment of the new weapon. The relatively flat trajectory of cannonballs made sweeping, horizontal fire most effective, and high walls and towers lost most of their defensive advantages. The silhouettes of fortresses became lower, as the traditional vertical defense shifted toward a horizontal one. The cannon's first victim was the tower whose height was gradually reduced until, toward the end of the century, it was generally cut off at walltop level (*Figs. 53–54*). The walls themselves remained relatively high to prevent escalade, but they were now set into a wide, deep ditch from which only their upper parts projected (*Figs. 57–58*). This not only permitted the installation of defensive batteries a few feet above ground level, but had the additional advantage of offering a smaller target to the enemy's guns. Early efforts to make walls more resistent to cannon fire led to a strong battering of their lower surfaces (*Fig. 48*) and to backing them with earthen terraces.[42]

This transitional phase, during which military architecture groped its way toward a new approach to fortification, produced a bewildering variety of tentative solutions, many of them so handsome in their carefully proportioned, massive plasticity that they must rank high among the most beautiful functional structures ever built. Most of the experiments were made on the relatively small scale of individual forts and castles, as cities seemingly preferred to await positive results before resorting to large-scale and expensive reconstructions of their enceintes. The castle of Soncino, built for Galeazzo Maria Sforza in 1473, still appears medieval in its general aspect (*Fig. 49*). But the towers have been lowered and the walls battered, and on one of its four corners stands a unique experimental tower that has two levels of machicolations instead of the normal one (*Fig. 50*). When Francesco di Giorgio fortified the duchy of Urbino for Federigo da Montefeltro between 1477 and 1482, he experimented with a polygonal tower at Mondovia (*Fig. 51*), an oval one at Cagli (*Fig. 52*), and round ones at San Leo (*Fig. 53*).[43] Equally plastic forms were used by Baccio Pontelli in his elegant fort at Ostia Antica; built in 1485 to protect the now shifted mouth of the Tiber, this *rocca* summarizes the state which military architecture had reached toward the end of the century (*Fig. 54*). The high *mastio*, or keep, is a medieval remnant, as are the machicoulis galleries, which had lost their purpose by this time, but which proved to be an extremely tenacious feature.[44] But the main structure is relatively low, the towers have been cut off at curtain level, and fully casemated gun emplacements (among the first of their kind) have been placed near the base of the walls to permit a sweeping defense of the ditch with horizontal fire.[45]

Most of these changes were modifications of traditional fortification methods, and, while they permitted a more effective use of defensive weapons, they did not answer the most serious problem raised by the cannon. Before the end of the century it became evident that no masonry walls, no matter how strongly built or reinforced, could withstand the repeated impact of iron cannonballs. This fact was most forcefully impressed upon the Italians by Charles

VIII's campaign in Italy to assert his claim to the throne of Naples in 1494, when French artillery was able to reduce even the best and strongest medieval walls within a matter of hours.[46] The disaster made it clear that only the most radical change in fortification design, and the complete abandonment of past approaches, could lead to a solution that might offer the defenders the hope of successfully resisting a cannon-led siege.[47] The urgency with which the problem was viewed is indicated by the fact that not only military men, but artists, architects, and humanistic scholars eagerly applied themselves to the task of finding an answer to the threat of the cannon. The nimblest and most ingenious minds of the period, including Francesco di Giorgio, Leonardo da Vinci, and Michelangelo, set out to solve a problem that, to them, must have had the additional appeal of an intellectual challenge that might yield to rational analysis.

The eventual solution might have been very different if Italian architects had adopted the northern method of constructing ramparts in tamped earth. The advantages of earthen fortifications, their ability to resist bombardment by absorbing cannonballs rather than being shattered by them, were well known and had strong advocates in the south, but Italian architects preferred to build in brick and stone.[48] Their arguments against earth construction, centered upon its lack of permanence due to weathering and the rotting of reinforcing timbers, seemed cogent enough; but one feels that, at least partly, they were inspired by an instinctive preference for masonry construction which was rooted in a centuries-old tradition reaching back into antiquity. In Italy, earthen ramparts were never considered to be more than mere temporary expedients that were to be replaced by permanent stone work at the earliest opportunity. This seemingly unbending and tradition-bound conservatism of Italian architects turned out to be one of the major springboards for the development of an entirely new and revolutionary system of fortification that was eagerly adopted by the entire civilized world and proved to be effective down to the nineteenth century.

Italian architects conceded that their stone walls could not resist cannon fire. Since they were unwilling to sacrifice their traditional construction methods, they set out to find the means which would permit them to seal off the inevitable breach. Two methods proved to be effective. One of these consisted in backing the threatened part of a wall with a high earthen rampart (*retirata*) which served as a secondary wall and as a platform for artillery firing frontally and point-blank through the breach (*Fig. 55*). But even more effective was flanking fire close to and parallel with the outside of the walls. If artillery were placed on platforms projecting from the walls, any breach between two neighboring platforms could be sealed off from the outside by decimating the assaulting enemy forces with enfilading fire before they reached the breach proper. This latter discovery led to the development of the bastioned defensive rings which became known and admired as the "Italian method" and served as the standard system of fortification for the next three centuries.

Towers which projected from fortress walls had been built for more than two millennia and they had been recommended by Vitruvius, the oracle of Renaissance architects, whose treatise must have been known to most Italian planners of the late fifteenth and sixteenth centuries. Thus, Renaissance engineers merely had to adapt an age-old principle to the greater range and power of the cannon; but the most practical shape and size of these projecting, cannon-bearing platforms, and the ideal distance from one to the other became the subjects of heated debates and long and varied experimentation. During the late fifteenth and early sixteenth centuries round towers were in wide use, as they were believed to offer the best resistance to enemy fire. With Vitruvius, it was argued that the round shape was inherently the strongest and that missiles, in this case cannonballs, tended to glance off rather than shatter its rounded surfaces.

The Veronese architect Fra Giocondo used such rounded forms when he fortified Treviso (*Figs. 56, 58–59*) and Padua (*Fig. 57*) for Venice during that Republic's war against the League of Cambrai. When Venice found herself unprepared to meet the League's aggression, she decided to sacrifice her cities on the mainland, with the exception of Treviso. This town was to be held at all costs to serve as the future base of operations for the reconquest of lost territories. In June, 1509, Fra Giocondo was entrusted with the task of converting the city into a fortress. He found a town with a medieval core that was enclosed by dilapidated walls and surrounded by sprawling suburbs which contained the best public and private buildings and housed the majority of the city's population.

The Veronese friar's recipe for rendering the city defensible was farsighted, drastic, and extremely unpopular.[49] He decided to utilize the medieval walls as best he could, but to enlarge the enceinte in proportion with the availability of manpower and of defensive weapons. His most controversial decision was to raze all buildings within a 500 meter belt in front of the new defensive line, in order to deprive the enemy of cover and give the defenders a clear field of fire. Since many citizens stood to lose their best and most comfortable residences, Fra Giocondo's plan met with violent opposition, and the Venetian Senate needed several months and all of its persuasiveness to pacify the rebellious population and convince it of the urgent need for the proposed measures.

Work was finally begun in November of 1509. The medieval enclosure was enlarged by about one fourth and its outline regularized to form a rough rectangle. The old walls were utilized whenever possible; they were lowered, backed up with massive earthen terraces, and reinforced with projecting, semicircular artillery platforms constructed in tamped earth; old towers were cut down to the level of the new ramparts. Fra Giocondo added the final touch to his impressive fortifications with hydraulic works which permitted the raising of the water level in the ditches and the partial flooding of the outside terrain to a distance of about 1 mile. Work was pushed through energetically against all obstacles and, in October, 1511, Treviso's new defenses could prove their efficiency against a League army that came to invest the city. After several fruitless assaults, the siege was lifted and the enemy retired, as the task of conquering the town was deemed too difficult.

As was Italian custom, Treviso's earthen defenses were encased in masonry shirts as soon as the most immediate danger to the city had passed. While it cannot be proven with certainty, it is highly probable that the extant fortifications closely reflect the original forms that were designed by Fra Giocondo in 1509. His uncompromising and progressive style is shown best by the northern part of the enceinte which is still fairly well preserved (*Figs. 58, 59*). All halfway measures are shunned by the architect who, on a sweeping scale and with great consequence, designed a defensive system that, for the first time, fully conforms with the new principle of horizontal defense. The walls are perhaps the lowest built during the entire sixteenth century; rising from the bottom of a wide ditch, they are barely 6 meters high; and less than half their height projected above the rim of the counterscarp. Gun embrasures in the artillery platforms are placed low and close to the curtains, permitting the defenders to protect both ditch and walls with flanking fire. And the generosity with which the interior terraces have been laid out is truly surprising (*Fig. 59*); the combined width of terrace and *pomoerium* exceeds 50 meters and must have assured easy and efficient movement of men and heavy equipment; and the wide *pomoerium* provided ample space for the construction of *retirate* if they were needed (*Fig. 56*). The Treviso defenses are "modern" in almost all respects, and only the round artillery platforms give them the stamp of the transitional phase of fortification.[50]

Despite their greater structural strength, and their evident efficiency during the Treviso siege, round bastions suffered from a number of disadvantages. One of these was the dead angle at their immediate fronts which could not be adequately protected by flanking fire from adjacent bastions. This defect is graphically illustrated by Gabrio Busca with a drawing (*Fig. 60*) in which he criticizes Dürer's system of fortification. Also, the round platform limited the defenders' potential fire power, as only one, at most two, cannon would be positioned to sweep the surface of the adjacent curtain effectively. Finally, cannon placed radially around a circular perimeter produced scattered fire, and no more than two or three guns could be brought to bear on any given point on the plain before them.

Most of these difficulties were solved when military architects adopted the triangle as the basic shape of their bastions. The triangular head of the bastion was connected with the curtain by means of short wall sections, the "flanks," where up to four cannon could be installed for the protection of each curtain. At the same time, the slanting surfaces of the angular front could be fully protected from neighboring bastions, as well as from parts of the curtains (*Fig. 61*). These flanking batteries became the most important and sensitive feature of the new system of fortification. Their protection against enemy fire was a major concern of military architects and led to the design of projecting bastion shoulders (orillions) and the typical, although not universal, arrowhead plan of the sixteenth-century bastion.

The solution had been approached, notably in a pentagonal fort built at Città Castellana by Giuliano da Sangallo and Antonio da Sangallo the Elder around 1495, but the new system had never been fully realized before 1501. In that year, Antonio da Sangallo the Elder, with a probable assist from his brother Giuliano, built a small fort near the beach at Nettuno that may be regarded as the military equivalent of Bramante's Tempietto in Rome, as it also ushers in a new era in the history of architecture.[51] The Nettuno fort is the first military structure in which the possibilities of bastioned defenses have been fully explored and where, on a small scale, a brand new theory of fortification has found practical application (*Figs. 62, 63*). Guns installed in the withdrawn flanks of triangular bastions can protect not only the curtains, but also the slanted faces of neighboring bastions. A complement of only eight men stationed at the flanks can keep the fort's periphery under complete surveillance, as there are no blind spots left within the closed defensive system; all surfaces can be seen and be defended with interlacing lanes of fire. At Nettuno only the very high walls, which rise from the ditch to a height of over 20 meters, remain archaic; but plan and elevation of a structure do not necessarily go hand in hand, and one can remain old-fashioned while the other is revolutionary. Toward mid-century the salient features of the Nettuno plan will be fused with Fra Giocondo's elevations to produce the final and effective answer to the threat of the cannon.

The new bastion type did not find immediate general acceptance. Bramante still used the round forms of the transitional style in 1508 when he built his fortress at the harbor of Civitàvecchia and made a final effort to counter the power of artillery with massive masonry. And where the triangular bastion was adopted, it was at first subject to as much experimentation as the tower had been some decades earlier. The Baluardo Pispini (*Fig. 64*) continues the line of picturesque experimental solutions that reaches back to mid-fifteenth century. It is the only remaining one of several bastions with which Baldassare Peruzzi, beginning 1528, strengthened the medieval walls of his native Siena. Over 12 meters high and extremely blunt-nosed, its somewhat cramped flanks have three gun levels; the heaviest artillery was installed in the vault-covered top level and had to be supplied awkwardly by hoists through the bastion's open back. On the other hand, its nicely proportioned, plastic quality is reminiscent of Francesco di Giorgio's forms and bespeaks the hand of the artist-architect who felt it necessary to provide his structure with the finishing touch of a decorative cornice. A very different approach is shown in a bastion which Antonio da Sangallo the Younger built in the 1530's and which, bare of all architectural niceties, forcefully expresses its military function. This bastion near the Porta Ardeatina (*Fig. 65*) is the only one that was completed for Pope Paul III's ambitious but abortive project to refortify Rome. Its generous dimensions and massive parapets, its powerfully armed flanks, and the subterranean corridors with their antimining listening chambers made it an admired standard for generations of later military architects.

Some twenty years earlier, Antonio had already shown that an entire city can be ringed with bastions of the new type to form a defensive system that had no blind spots. In 1515, using Bramante's fortress as the southern anchor, he surrounded Civitàvecchia and its harbor with bastions of varying shapes, so designed that all their faces could be protected from neighboring flanks (*Fig. 66*). In this earliest partially extant bastioned enceinte,[52] Antonio, systematically and with exacting logic, applied to a long, irregular trace the system that had been used for the first time by his uncles in the small Nettuno fort. With it he proved that the new system could be used effectively in urban fortification and that, in fact, it was more efficient for large enceintes than for small individual fortresses.

Only parts of the two northern-most bastions of the Civitàvecchia enceinte still stand today; both are rather pointed and would have been criticized by later engineers who preferred bastions with blunt leading edges, claiming that they would be less easily ruined by enemy fire. A bastion from the Ferrara enceinte, built during the last phase of that city's century-long refortification efforts, illustrates the type that was favored by military architects during the second half of the sixteenth century (*Fig. 67*). Large, massive, blunt-nosed, it is crouched behind the counterscarp like a panther ready to leap at his enemies. It is a long step indeed that military architecture has taken from the fragile elegance of Peruzzi's bastion to this powerful monster that exudes the cool functionalism of the engineer's art. Ferrara's enceinte is like a history book on sixteenth-century fortification in which all developmental stages are illustrated, from the transitional round-towered forms to this late model which was the near-standard type of a mature bastion.[53]

The Ferrara enceinte also is one of the very few that has preserved a small part of its counterscarp and glacis. These advanced works became more and more important as the range of the cannon increased; they were the means by which the defenders tried to keep the enemy as far as possible from the magistral line. Sloping down and outward from the rim of the counterscarp, the glacis was designed so that only the breastworks of bastions and curtains would be visible to an enemy approaching from the field, thus giving his artillery a minimum target, while, at the same time, keeping him exposed to the defenders who had a clear field of vision down the artificial slope. Since pointblank horizontal fire was the most efficient with a solid shot, the walls of a fortress became vulnerable to an enemy only if he could install his breaching batteries on the rim of the counterscarp, as shown in Figure 68. To get there, however, he had to dig his way laboriously up the sloping glacis through zig-zag trenches while under the grazing fire of the defenders. And even after breaching a wall, his assault forces had to brave the withering cross fire from the bastion flanks before they reached the breach and, after they had stormed it, the frontal fire from the *retirata.*

Sieges became drawn out and costly. But so did the preparations to withstand them, and the replacement of ancient fortifications with a modern bastioned enceinte could severely strain a city's, or even a small state's, economic resources. Few cities were either able or willing to finance such monumental projects, and most cities, like Reims (*Fig. 69*), would resort to half-measures in the hope that they might suffice to bring old walls up to modern standards. Such renovations usually consisted in backing medieval walls with earthen terraces, and in strengthening them with projecting artillery plat-forms at strategic points. Augsburg (Fig. 70) did not go much be-yond such measures in the initial "modernization" of its walls. Eventually it decided to protect the most easily accessible side of the city with modern, bastioned defenses, a decision that may have been partly inspired by an anticipated urban expansion in that di-rection. Under such circumstances, and because the new fortifica-tions were only earthworks, the cost of the project may have ap-peared bearable to the citizens.

Similar stop-gap measures were planned by Lucca's city council in 1545, when it entrusted Jacopo Seghizzi with the modernization of its medieval fortifications. Seghizzi, who, at the time, was work-ing on the Pesaro fortifications for Duke Guidobaldo II of Urbino, was released from that project just long enough to prepare some designs for Lucca. His plans were handicapped from the start by the council's decision that he must utilize the old walls as much as possible, and, since Guidobaldo refused to release his architect to Lucca on a permanent basis, work progressed very slowly. In 1561 the progressive members of the city council finally prevailed and it was decided to build a brand-new defensive ring under the direction of Luca Paciotto.[54] The result was one of the most impressive bas-tioned enceintes extant (Figs. 71–74), and one that assured Lucca's independence down to the nineteenth century.[55] Designed by an ex-pert fully versed in the latest theories on fortification, all parts of the enceinte are beautifully flanked from spacious, open battery em-placements that eliminated vexing ventilation problems (Fig. 72); the bastions are low, wide, blunt, and protect their flanks with massive orillions (Fig. 73); they, in turn, were shielded by a glacis dotted with ravelins and lunettes, of which a few still survive on the town's northern front (Fig. 74).

No matter how successful, however, the refortification of older cities always fell short of the ideal solutions propounded by six-teenth-century military architects. The perfect fortification belt en-visioned by them was a regular polygon with blunt evenly spaced bastions at intervals adjusted to the current range of artillery, which could be surrounded with an impenetrable wall of defensive fire created by tightly interlacing firelanes. This kind of symmetry could rarely be achieved in the refortification of developed urban bodies, and even an enceinte as well conceived and executed as Lucca's had to be a compromise. Its irregular trace demanded constant ad-justment of bastion shapes and intervals and forced the designer to make concessions to site and existing conditions that were in con-flict with his theoretical ideals. Lucca's north front, for instance, where the old walls were used in the early stages of the refortification project, must always have seemed to be a weak link in an otherwise solid defensive chain.

But even under conditions that were not ideal, the bastion had been developed into so powerful a defensive weapon that, by the middle of the sixteenth century, the curtains had become almost impregnable. While the walls could still be breached, the withering cross fire from the two flanking bastions made any assault upon the breach suicidal. As a result, the attackers began to shift their offensive efforts toward the bastions themselves, which had become the least heavily protected parts of the defensive system. But if the bastion was the most vulnerable part of a city's defenses, it was also its potentially most powerful offensive weapon. Its triangular platform served the dual purpose of protecting the flanks and of being the base of operations from which the defenders attempted to disrupt the enemy's assault preparations. Usually siege operations were concentrated on one or two bastions only. As soon as the enemy's direction of attack was evident, it became imperative to supply the endangered bastion with all available artillery, as the besieged would attempt to match or exceed the fire power of the attacking forces. Some cities owned up to two hundred cannon, according to Francesco de Marchi; but what good are two hundred cannon, he writes, if they cannot be brought to bear on the enemy?[56]

The shifting of artillery from bastion to bastion must indeed have presented a problem of the first magnitude, as it involved the movement, by primitive means, of pieces weighing up to 15,000 pounds. This called for straight and wide access roads with manageable slopes which linked the bastions with the interior of the fortress and along which threatened sectors of the defensive system could be supplied and reinforced quickly and efficiently. Such ideal conditions, however, could rarely be achieved when old cities were to be refortified, as they would have required major and intolerable surgical incisions into the urban fabric. The ideal could be realized only in the new military foundations with which the rulers of newly emerging national states fortified their borders against their neighbors. Here the new defensive theories not only could be developed to their full potential, but they could be combined with the equally revolutionary radial city plan which was ideally suited to their needs.

The radial city plan made its first, tentative appearance in a treatise by Antonio Filarete around 1465 (*Fig. 75*). Filarete, however, was not able to convert his mental concept into graphic terms, as he used rectangular units for his complex of central piazze which he could not integrate with the envisioned radial street network. Francesco di Giorgio first produced practicable designs some twenty years later, when he adjusted the shape of his central piazza to that of the city's polygonal circumference (*Fig. 76*). With this step Francesco created the prototype which, with variations, was developed into a polished instrument of military precision by later generations of engineers and architects.[57]

The combination of bastioned fortifications with the radial city plan was put to its first practical test not in Italy, but in France by an Italian architect. During fifty years of spasmodic warfare between France and the Imperium, towns along the Franco-Imperial border were razed and rebuilt repeatedly. When warfare came to a temporary halt in 1544 and the antagonists decided to adjust their boundaries, France lost the town of Stenay on the right bank of the Meuse. To offset this loss, Francis I ordered the construction of a new fortress town on that river's left bank, Villefranche-sur-Meuse. Its planner and military architect was the Bolognese engineer Girolamo Marini. Chastillon's view of the city (*Fig. 77*) shows that its basic shape was a square, the four corners of which were fortified with huge triangular bastions. From the large central "place d'armes" eight streets radiate outward, four toward bastions, and four toward the curtain centers. Although transverse ring streets are lacking, this is, in fact, the earliest application of the new urban scheme to a modern fortification system and, probably, the first realization of a complete radial city plan in the history of urbanism.

Some ten years later the Dutch architect Sebastian van Noyen built Philippeville for Philip II of Spain near today's French-Belgian border (*Fig. 78*). Its shape was a pentagon which, according to contemporary military theory, represented an advance over the square of Villefranche. In designing their defensive rings, sixteenth-century military architects generally worked with two modules: the size of the flanks, which had to accommodate at least two cannon side-by-side, and the length of the curtain. Both varied according to the opinions of individual planners. Some insisted that the flanks be spacious enough to allow the lateral installation of three, or even four, cannon with their crews. Their advocated curtain lengths varied between 200 and 500 meters, depending in part upon the caliber of the defensive artillery to be used. But once a designer had arrived at a combination of values which he considered to be ideal, he would use it as the basic unit of measurement for the entire fortress plan. Depending upon the area to be fortified, the unit could be multiplied at will, creating many-sided polygons in which each additional side added to the space enclosed. In fact, cost estimates for fortification projects were often expressed in terms of costs for one bastion and one adjoining curtain only, leaving it up to the state or potentate to multiply the figure by the number of units needed to surround a given area. A third consideration that had to be taken into account was the shape of the bastion, which was to be as blunt as possible. Unfortunately it was not always possible to combine a blunt-nosed bastion with the ideal curtain length and flank dimensions, and it became the designer's task to strive for an acceptable compromise. The fewer the angles of the basic fortress shape, the more difficult was the solution (*Fig. 79*). For this reason, the square was generally condemned as one of the geometric figures which lent itself least to efficient fortification. Still, almost all treatises on military architecture showed at least one example of a fortified square, since it represented the smallest, and therefore cheapest, fortress that could be built. But even for small fortresses the pentagon was generally preferred, while polygons of from seven to twelve sides were usually considered best for larger enclosures.

Military architects eagerly adopted the radial city plan when they realized that it greatly enhanced the potential strength of their ideal enceintes by providing them with an extremely efficient system of interior communications. It permitted the key points of the defensive system, the bastions, to be linked with each other and with the town's center by means of straight and unimpeded traffic arteries. The central piazza could serve as the mustering point and the dispersal center for the city's military strength which could be channeled to any part of the defensive ring quickly and efficiently. Also, since each bastion could be seen from the central piazza, a commander stationed on a tower or raised platform in its center was in complete control of the city's defenses, able to shift his forces at will and according to need. In short, the advantages of the radial street plan to the new system of fortification were so obvious that most theoretical treatises did not even feel it necessary to comment upon them. And the plan's almost universal acceptance among military architects is attested by Antonio Lupicini, whose only reference to the street plan of the ideal city in his treatise (*Fig. 80*) is the dry comment that it has been laid out "as it is done in modern fortification."[58]

In fusing bastioned fortifications with the radial-city plan, the military architect converted into a functional tool a plan that had embodied the ideals of Renaissance urbanism. He not only trimmed it of all symbolic and most aesthetic qualities, but even disregarded the needs of the civilian populations that were to inhabit his projected fortress cities. On many theoretical designs the citizen was not even accorded the right of easy access to his town, as the traffic system was oriented toward the bastions and the town gates were designed like posterns to serve military sorties rather than civilian traffic. To most military planners the inhabitants of a town represented no more than a manpower pool from which the commander could draw additional forces to augment his garrison in case of need. From this point of view, large cities were considered to be stronger than small ones, as a more numerous population could furnish a greater number of defenders.

This seems to have been one of the considerations when Venice decided, in 1593, to protect its eastern frontiers against the threat of Turkish aggression. Palmanova (*Figs. 81–86*) was to be the largest and most powerful fortress in the world and the original project called for a town with twelve bastions. Economic considerations eventually forced the Venetian Senate to cut this number to nine, which represented a 25 percent reduction in both the size and the cost of the project. But even in this shrunken condition, Palmanova remained the largest military town in its time, and the only radial city to be built in Italy during the sixteenth century.

Usually misattributed to Vincenzo Scamozzi, Palma's original plan undoubtedly was of the utilitarian military type and designed either by Giulio Savorgnano, the then-ruling dean of Venetian military architects, or by his assistant Bonaiuto Lorini.[59] Among several anonymous designs for the Palma project which have survived, the one shown in Figure 83 represents the military ideal in its most frigidly functional severity. Nine master streets depart from the corners of the nine-sided central piazza and lead straight for their respective bastions. Secondary streets lead toward curtain centers, but are cut off from them, as well as from the piazza, by building strips. In his overwhelming concern for the plan's utilitarian, military aspects, the designer did not even bother to provide his city with gates. Savorgnano might well have thought in these terms, for we are told that the gates on his lost master model for the city were hidden in the shadows of bastions and, thus, were offset from the street system. The extreme and almost crude functionalism of such designs must have shocked Marcantonio Barbaro, the project's first general supervisor, who was a lawyer, humanist, and friend of such men as Veronese, Palladio, and Scamozzi.

Another, probably later, design for the Palma project (*Fig. 84*) shows that some significant modifications were introduced into the sterile military plan, presumably at Barbaro's urging. In its essentials it is very similar to an ideal plan which Lorini published in his treatise and may represent one of the final versions which he and Savorgnano submitted for Senate approval.[60] It makes concessions to the needs of the town's inhabitants by conveniently placing three gates into curtain centers and by providing traffic dispersal areas in the form of small squares placed midway between gates and the civic center. But the plan retains all those features which military engineers considered essential: the access roads are cut off by the innermost ring of houses which acts as an effective screen between gates and central piazza; and above all, every one of the bastions is connected with the central piazza by means of a straight and unimpeded traffic artery. The plan also retains one of the most characteristic and universal features of sixteenth-century military designs in the form of the central piazza: it is nine-sided, like the town's circumference, and the master streets radiate outward from its corners.

This was the extent to which the military planner was willing to make concessions to civilian needs. But the Palma plan was subjected to additional changes which were considered ruinous by Lorini and are severely criticized by him in his treatise. A late-seventeenth-century plan of Palmanova as it was actually built (*Fig. 85*) shows that the shape of the central piazza was changed to a hexagon. It is entered through its sides, rather than its corners, and of the six radial master streets only three point toward bastions, while the remaining three run straight toward the town gates. This means that six of the nine bastions were isolated from the city's center, a decision which no sixteenth-century military engineer in his right mind could have accepted. Only an architect who placed civilian above military needs could have introduced such features which so radically affected the town's military efficiency. It seems ironical that the military architect, after almost a century's planning for an occasion just as this, was prevented from turning his theories into practice by what must have been massive civilian interference. If Scamozzi claims in his treatise that he "did many things too numerous to mention" at Palma,[61] he may well have meant that his friend Barbaro gave him a free hand to mutilate the original military plans for the town. In effect, Palma the fortress was emasculated in a futile attempt to create Palma the city.[62]

The Palma miscarriage may have been partly responsible for the military architect's eventual loss of interest in the radial plan. Heinrich Schickhardt, who was personally acquainted with Lorini and probably knew of his friend's problems at Palmanova, shunned the radial plan when he was commissioned by Duke Frederik of Wuerttemberg to build a colonial town in the Black Forest. Instead, Schickhardt found his inspiration in Dürer's ideal plan (*Fig. 87*) and all of his designs for Freudenstadt are rectangular patterns inscribed into squares (*Fig. 88*). And a hundred years later, when Vauban built his most famous fortress of Neuf-Brisach, he used a neat but standard checkerboard plan inside his powerfully fortified octagon (*Fig. 89*).

Sebastien le Prestre, Marquis de Vauban, whose name became a legend, dominated the field of military engineering during the second half of the seventeenth century. Louis XIV's favorite military architect (until he dared to criticize the King's tax system), Vauban is said to have built or rebuilt some 160 strongholds and to have surrounded France with a cordon of powerful fortresses. Although he was one of the most prolific builders of fortifications in the history of military architecture, Vauban's contemporary fame rested primarily upon his legendary achievements as a siege engineer and the repute that no fortress could withstand a Vauban-led assault. His successes in this field were due largely to his famed "system of parallels," a logical and systematic refinement of past siege methods which enabled him to advance his siege artillery in a series of carefully calculated and methodically executed movements, under the protection of trenches dug parallel to the defensive lines, until his breaching batteries were securely established at the counterscarp. Vauban's treatise on the subject (*Traité des sièges et de l'attaque des places*) went through several editions and became the standard handbook for eighteenth-century siege engineers.

As a designer of fortifications, Vauban modified the "Italian system" by adjusting it to the increased range of artillery. At Neuf-Brisach, Vauban's most mature work, the trace of the bastioned magistral line remains essentially unchanged (*Figs. 90–91*). But the bastions are no longer the dominant feature of the defensive system; they have shrunk to relative insignificance, as they are dwarfed by the enormous outworks which have been built into a ditch that is over 100 meters wide.[63] Practically enveloped by their lunettes, the bastions have lost most of their former function of being the chief defenses of the curtains. Instead, their main purpose now seems to be that of backing up and protecting the lunettes in case they should be breached. The curtain proper is covered by a tenaille that has been inserted between it and a powerful double-ravelin which, on the design, appears to be the most potent element of the defensive system. In addition, and most significantly, Vauban has fortified the entire counterscarp, converting the covered way into a strongly armed first line of defense. Behind these enormously powerful outworks, which are all carefully executed in brick masonry, the magistral line looks rather puny and, in fact, has lost most of its former significance.

Once the bastion ceased to be the key to a city's defenses, the problem of supplying it along a straight access road lost its urgency and the radial plan, which had been the ideal of sixteenth-century planners, lost favor among later military architects. Like Vauban at

Neuf-Brisach, they preferred the less-complex checkerboard plan which is more easily organized and lends itself more readily to subdivision.

The defenses of Neuf-Brisach express, in well-developed form, a change in the theory of fortification. With the growing range and power of artillery, it became increasingly important for the defenders to keep the enemy as far away from the magistral line as possible. Accordingly the defenses were moved forward and the outworks strengthened to the point at which they could be expected to withstand the main brunt of an assault. The development is well illustrated by the successive growth stages of Palmanova's fortifications (*Figs 84–86*). In the late sixteenth century the bastioned enceinte with a wide ditch and a simple glacis was considered to be quite sufficient. Early during the seventeenth century these fortifications were strengthened with ravelins, which were built outside the ditch and in front of the curtains for their and the flank's additional protection. In the early nineteenth century, when Napoleon decided to make Palma the key to the eastern defenses of his "regno," its dilapidated fortifications were not only restored and modernized, but also provided with additional outworks in the form of lunettes placed in front of the bastions. This extended the glacis to some 350 meters beyond the bastions and the powerfully armed lunettes became semi-independent strong points.[64] By moving much of their armament into these semidetached outworks, the defenders gradually converted a linear defense into a defense in depth, and the magistral line lost much of its former importance. By the end of the eighteenth century it could be generally assumed that a town had been lost once the enemy had crossed the glacis and established himself on the rim of the counterscarp.

As complex as the fortifications of Neuf-Brisach and those of Palmanova in their latest stage may seem, compared with the elaborate designs of other fortresses, they remained relatively conservative. Military architects, especially in the northern countries, seemingly tried to outdo each other in the invention of new and ever more complicated outworks. Demi-lunes, tenailles, double-tenailles, horn works, crownworks, in addition to the basic ravelins and lunettes, sprouted around towns and fortresses in ever-greater profusion and near-fantastic complexity. Sprawling fortification belts, many hundreds of meters wide and often dwarfing the areas of the cities they protected, became a dominant feature of the eighteenth-century landscape. They also constituted the last and most effective restraint on urban sprawl as, certainly, no civilian construction was tolerated within the confines of the glacis; nor was it likely to be permitted along its outer edge. When Palmanova was refortified,

Napoleon ordered three entire nearby villages to be razed so as to give the defenders a clear field of fire.

Low and hidden behind artificial slopes that rendered them next to invisible from the field, the outworks in these wide strips of no-man's land were visually far less imposing than ancient or medieval enceintes and, thus, were less likely to inspire the feeling of civic pride which earlier generations had felt for their urban walls. On the contrary, they may well have had an adverse psychological effect by producing a feeling of confinement and isolation in the enclosed populations. Where formerly a single gateway had separated the citizen from the countryside, he now had to traverse a quarter of a mile or more of barren, artificially shaped terrain before he reached the first fields. The Baroque glacis, perhaps, should be counted among the early man-made agents which, in growing numbers and with increased intensity since the advent of the industrial revolution, have contributed to the urban dweller's progressive alienation from his natural surroundings.

EPILOGUE

The proliferation of semidetached outworks, some of them so far removed from the magistral line that they became nearly independent strong points of the defense, represents the first step toward the eventual dissolution of continuous urban enceintes. During the nineteenth century, when the rifled gun-barrel enormously increased the range of artillery, and the explosive shell multiplied its striking power many fold, most traditional fortification methods became obsolete. They could no longer fulfill the primary purpose of fortification, which was to protect an urban center by keeping the enemy beyond the range at which he could either interrupt its economic life or harm its civilian population. To cope with the artillery's spectacular growth of power, the defenders were forced to increase the depth of their defenses by moving their strong points far out into the field. Cities were surrounded with small, but heavily armed fortresses which were strategically spaced so that all approaches to the town could be sealed off with tightly interlacing fire lanes. Since these forts had to be built at distances of several miles from the city proper, the construction of continuous fortification lines between them became impractical.

General Henri Brialmont, the "Belgian Vauban" of the nineteenth century, fortified Liège, Namur, and Antwerp in this manner. At Liège he ringed the town with heavily armed forts, built of concrete and mostly underground, at 2.5 mile intervals and at an average distance of 4 miles from the city.[65] Detached from each other and from their urban matrix, these nineteenth-century forts were largely self-sufficient and could function independently. And behind the invisible screen of their fire lanes, with which they protected each other and the city, the now purposeless urban enceintes could dissolve. The confining corset that had kept straining urban bodies in check for almost ten thousand years fell apart, and cities, bloated with the symptoms of incipient industrialism, spilled out into the countryside.

The demise of urban fortifications during the nineteenth century was hastened by the formation of centralized national states. Defenses could be transposed from individual urban bodies to territorial boundaries and only cities near national frontiers still needed to be fortified. Nevertheless, although expanded to protect entire nations, the old concept of fixed and permanent fortifications persisted: the trench warfare of the First World War was, essentially, only an adaptation to modern field warfare of ancient principles of fortification. And, during the 1930's, the Maginot and Siegfried Lines revived the age-old idea of fixed regional defenses that had already been put into practice by the Romans with the *limes* and by the Chinese with their Great Wall.

During the Second World War, the airplane's development to maturity added the third dimension to warfare. Defensive methods had to be modified again, but their underlying theory remained unchanged. Efforts continued to be concentrated upon ways and means of keeping a nation's urban and industrial centers out of the enemy's reach, and of protecting the civilian population. Cities and industrial complexes were ringed with anti-aircraft batteries and interceptor bases in the vain hope of protecting them against hostile aerial incursions. During the 1940's it became obvious that a nation could not shield its heartland against an enemy's air armadas if the attacks were pressed home with sufficient effort and regardless of losses. Raids could be made costly to the enemy but could not be prevented. Still, this did not really affect the validity of traditional defensive concepts, since it had been true throughout history that attacks, if carried out with sufficient force and intensity, could usually reduce a stronghold.

Only very recently, within the last decade or so, the final death blow was given to all past defensive concepts. Their irrevocable obsolescence was heralded by the appearance, during the last months of the Second World War, of the V-2 rocket, a weapon that could not be intercepted. Once its range and accuracy had been increased sufficiently, and it had been armed with the atomic warhead, its force became irresistible and the intercontinental ballistics missile has become what appears to be the ultimate offensive weapon. The expansion of national defensive systems to continental ones is futile, and the DEW line represents the last gasp of traditional concepts of defense. The ABM system is tantamount to mankind's confession that it has lost all hope of being able to protect itself. For the ABM system is an admission that neither cities, nor countries, nor continents can be defended; it is designed only to shield the weapons with which a country might hope to strike a retaliatory blow at the enemy. For the first time in history entire populations have become expendable, as the offense finally seems to have overwhelmed the defense after ten thousand years of fluctuating contest.

1. Jericho, wall and great tower, c. 7500
   B.C. View into the excavation ditch.
   Second worker from the top is standing on the remains of the round
   tower.

C   Courtyard
G   Granary
GR   Guardroom
P   Potter's workshops
W   Well
S   Shrine

2. Çatal Hüyük, plan of building level VI-B, c. 6000 B.C., after Mellaart.

3. Çatal Hüyük, reconstruction of section of level VI, after Mellaart.

4. Hacilar II-A, c. 5400 B.C. (center) and Hacilar I, c. 5250 B.C. (left and right), after
   Mellaart.

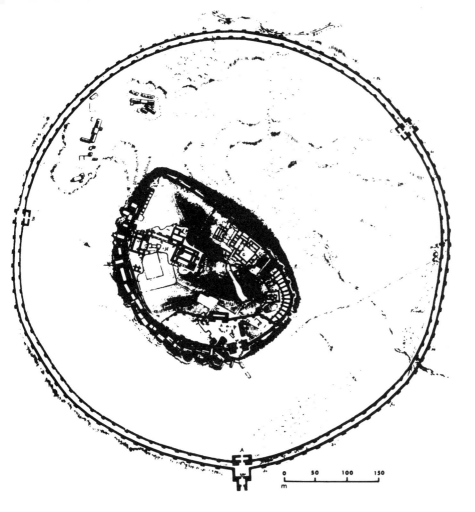

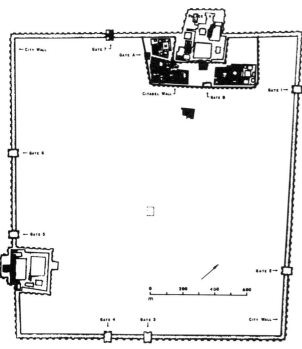

5. Zincirli, c. 1000 B.C.

6. Khorsabad (Dur-Sharrukin),
   c. 750 B.C.

7. Tiglath-pileser III attacking
   a city, from Nimrud, c. 740
   B.C.

8. Ashurnasirpal II besieging a
   city, from Nimrud, c. 870
   B.C.

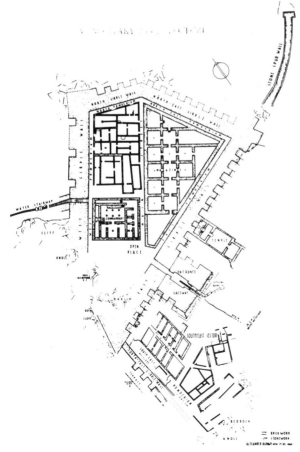

9. Fortress at Askut, Egypt, Middle Kingdom.

10. Fortress at Askut, reconstruction after Badawy.

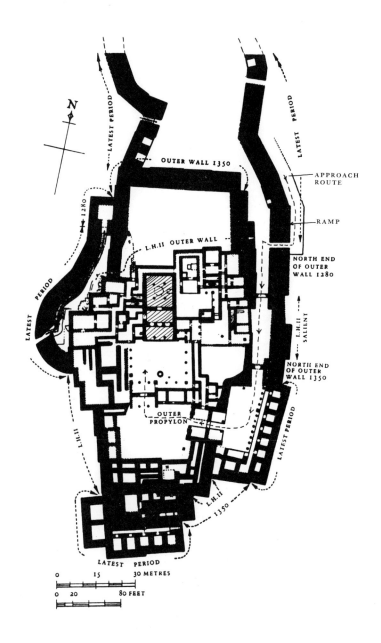

11. Tiryns, plan of southern part of the citadel, c. 1300 B.C. Shaded area in center is royal megaron. Fortified enclosure ("lower citadel") at top is only partly shown; dotted lines indicate walls' continuation.

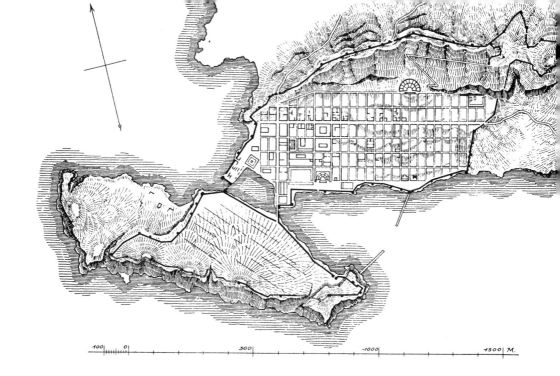

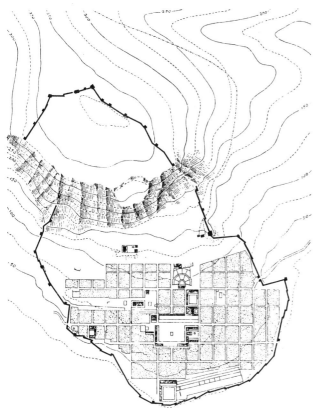

12. Knidos, fifth to fourth cen-
    tury B.C., after von Gerkan.

13. Priene, fourth century B.C.,
    after von Gerkan.

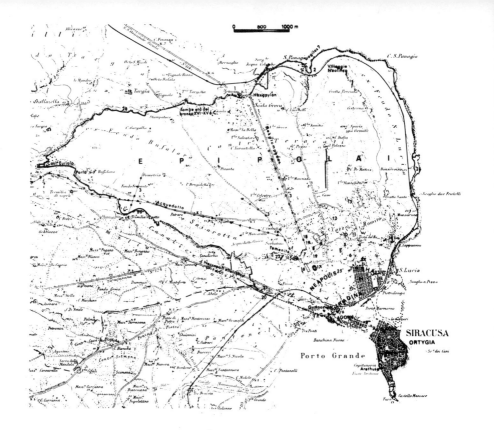

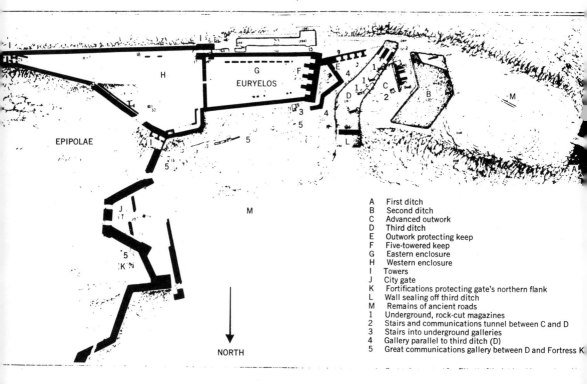

A	First ditch
B	Second ditch
C	Advanced outwork
D	Third ditch
E	Outwork protecting keep
F	Five-towered keep
G	Eastern enclosure
H	Western enclosure
I	Towers
J	City gate
K	Fortifications protecting gate's northern flank
L	Wall sealing off third ditch
M	Remains of ancient roads
1	Underground, rock-cut magazines
2	Stairs and communications tunnel between C and D
3	Stairs into underground galleries
4	Gallery parallel to third ditch (D)
5	Great communications gallery between D and Fortress K

NORTH

14. Syracuse, general plan, c. 400 B.C.

15. Syracuse, Castel Euryelos, plan, c. 400 B.C.

16. Syracuse, Castel Euryelos, keep and inner ditch, showing entrance to subterranean corridors.

17. Syracuse, Castel Euryelos, reconstruction after Mauceri.

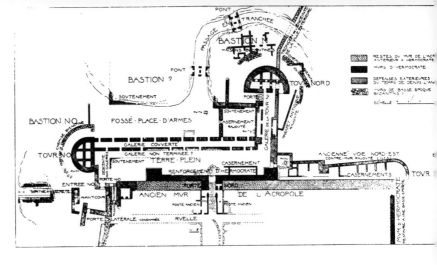

18. Selinus, defenses of the
    north front.

19. Selinus, reconstructed plan,
    c. 390 B.C.

20. Selinus, covered east-west gallery, looking north.

21. Selinus, reconstruction of the north front, after Krischen.

22. Miletus, general plan, c. 479 B.C., after von Gerkan.

23. Miletus, south front, c. 190 B.C.

24. Miletus, south wall, plan and elevation of gate and tower B.

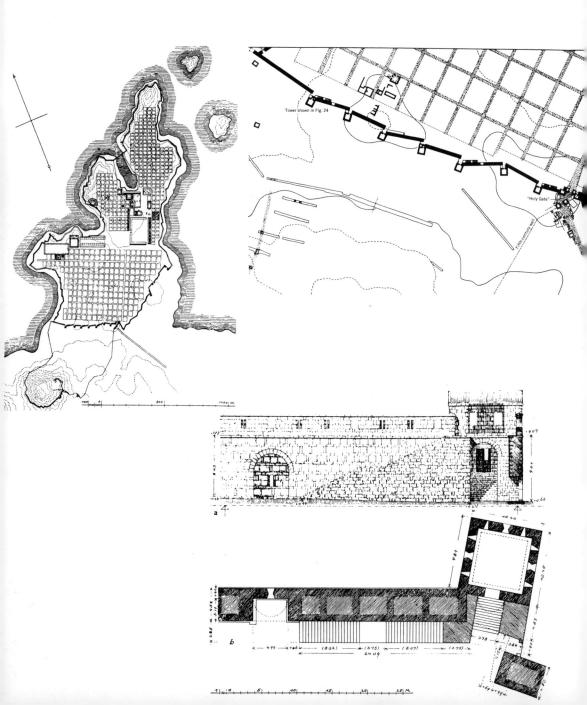

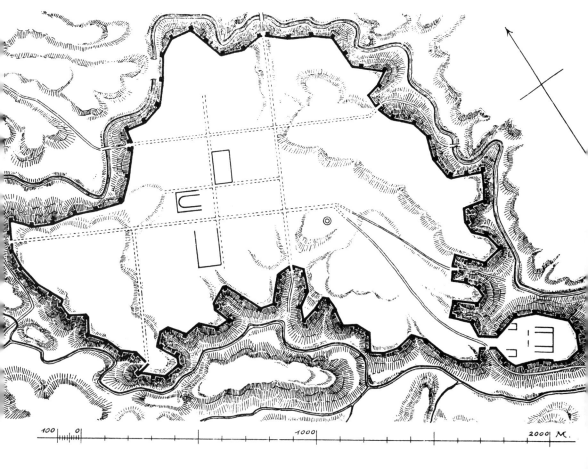

100 0   1000   2000 M.

25. Veii, fifth century B.C. (?), plan after von Gerkan.

26. Rosellae, north wall, sixth century B.C.

27. Orvieto, cliff on south side.

28. Orte, general view from the east.

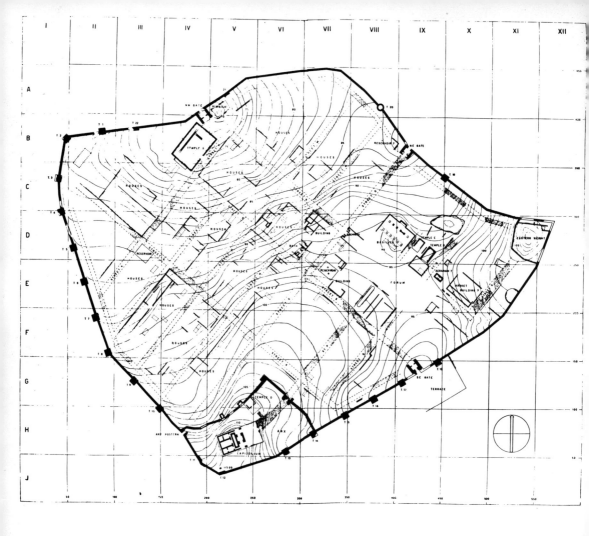

29. Cosa, plan, 273 B.C. The arx (sacred precinct), arx postern and capitolium are in the walled area at bottom.

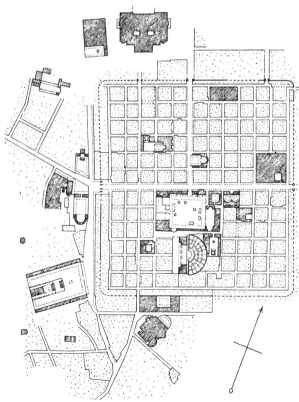

30. Cosa, polygonal wall and tower.

31. Timgad, plan, 100 A.D., after von Gerkan.

100 | | | | | | | | | 0 | | | 100 | | | 200 | | | 300 | M.

32. Spalato, c. 300 A.D., re-construction.

33. Rome, Porta Ostiensis, c. 400 A.D.

34. Rome, Aurelian wall, late third to early fifth century.

A   The great barbican
B   Gate of Narbonne
C   Gate of the aude
D   The great postern
E   Barbican of the castle
F   The castle
G   The church
H   The cloister
I   A courtyard
K   The hall
L   Entrance passage
M   The tower and the treasury
N   The moat of the castle
O   A lofty tower
P   Barbican of the postern
Q   Tower of the angle
R   Square tower
S   Ditch or moat of the city

TVXY   The lists between the inner
        and outer walls of enceinte or
        enclosure

35. Carcassonne, airview.

36. Carcassonne, c. 1285, plan
      after Viollet-le-Duc.

37. Carcassonne, Visigothic tower, c. 450 A.D., reconstruction after Viollet-le-Duc.

38. Carcassonne, wall with machicoulis gallery, c. 1130, reconstruction after Viollet-le-Duc.

A   A guard
B   A pioneer
C   The hoarding
D   The machicoulis
E   The platform for a passage
     inside the parapet

39. Medieval siege, with trebuchets in action, after
Viollet-le-Duc.

A The cat
B The pulley
C The catapult

D The crossbowmen
E The wooden tower
and drawbridge

40. Medieval siege, assault
from a siege tower, after
Viollet-le-Duc.

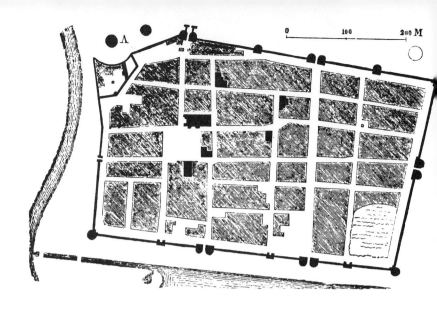

41. Aigues-Mortes, plan c. 1250.

42. Cittadella, 1220, airview.

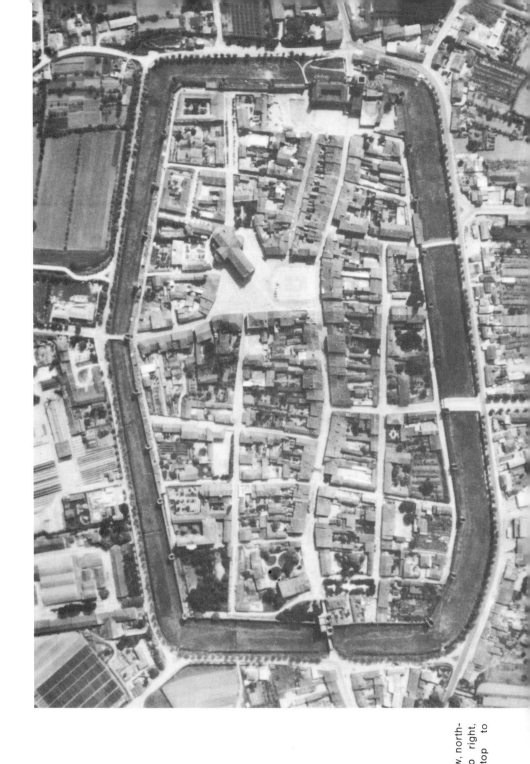

43. Montagnana, airview, north-south runs left to right, east-west runs top to bottom.

44. Montagnana, walls, c. 1360's.

45. Montagnana, interior of walls and *pomoerium*.

46. Montagnana, northwest gate (Rocca degli Alberi), 1360's.

47. Florence, plan showing successive enceintes, after Braunfels.

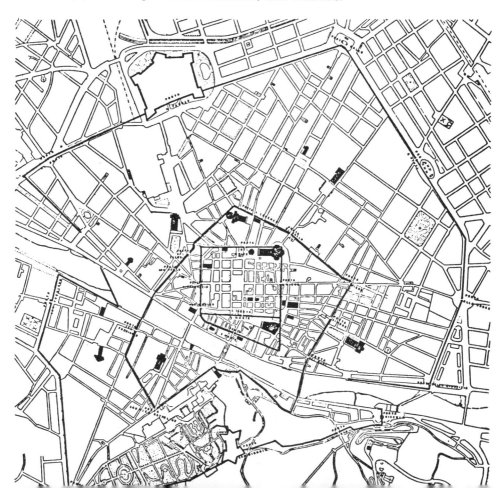

48. Iesi, town walls, 1480's, Baccio Pontelli (?).

49. Soncino, castello, 1473.

50. Soncino, castello,
    round corner tower.

51. Mondovia, polygonal tower
    of the Rocca, 1477–1482,
    Francesco di Giorgio.

52. Cagli, oval tower of former enceinte, 1477–1482, Francesco di Giorgio.

53. San Leo, outer fortifications, 1477–1482, Francesco di Giorgio (?).

54. Ostia Antica, 1485, Baccio Pontelli.

55. Siege, late
fifteenth or early
sixteenth century,
after Viollet-le-Duc.

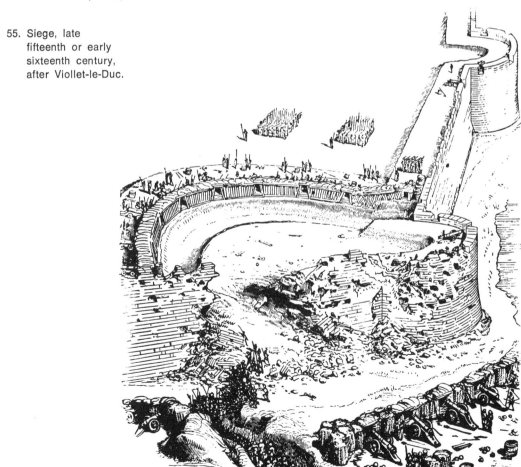

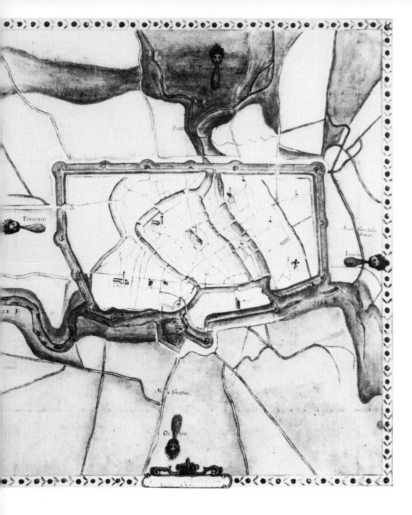

56. Treviso, plan by Caesare Malacreda, 1664, showing enceinte designed by Fra Giocondo.

57. Padua, ditch and walls, reflecting Fra Giocondo's work in 1509.

58. Treviso, ditch and exterior of wall, 1509, by Fra Giocondo.

59. Treviso, interior terrace and *pomoerium*.

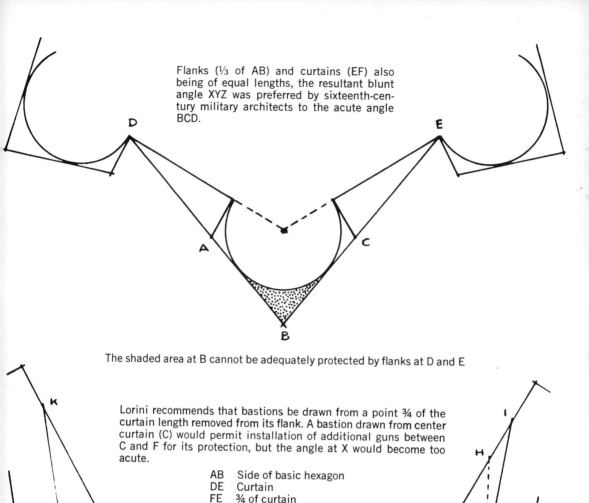

Flanks (⅓ of AB) and curtains (EF) also being of equal lengths, the resultant blunt angle XYZ was preferred by sixteenth-century military architects to the acute angle BCD.

The shaded area at B cannot be adequately protected by flanks at D and E

Lorini recommends that bastions be drawn from a point ¾ of the curtain length removed from its flank. A bastion drawn from center curtain (C) would permit installation of additional guns between C and F for its protection, but the angle at X would become too acute.

AB	Side of basic hexagon
DE	Curtain
FE	¾ of curtain
OP	Flank (⅓ of OQ)
PQ	Baseline of orillon
ET	"Length of defenses"

60. Comparison of round with triangular bastion, after G. Busca.

61. Construction of bastions for a hexagon, after B. Lorini.

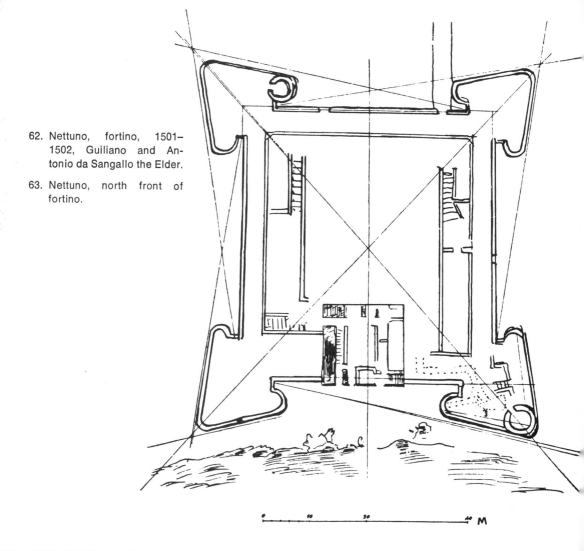

62. Nettuno, fortino, 1501–1502, Guiliano and Antonio da Sangallo the Elder.

63. Nettuno, north front of fortino.

64. Siena, Baluardo Pispini, 1530's, Baldassare Peruzzi.

65. Rome, Bastione Sangallo, 1537–1542,
    Antonio da Sangallo the Younger.

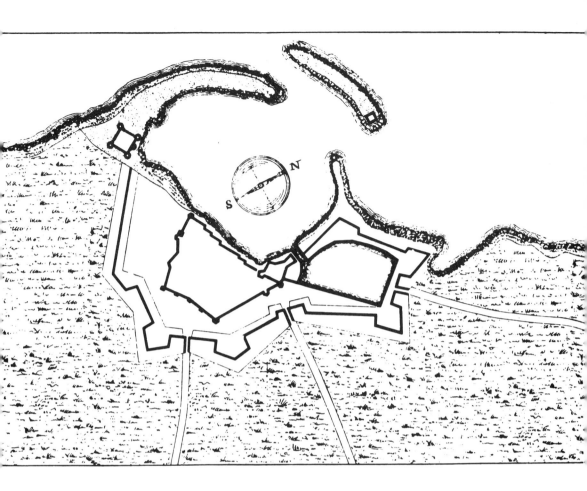

66. Civitavecchia, plan of enceinte, c. 1515, Antonio da Sangallo
the Younger. Bramante's fort is the square in upper left.

67. Ferrara, bastion, ditch, and counterscarp, 1559–1597.

A Bastions
B Breaching battery
C Inner rampart

68. Assault on a bastioned enceinte,
after Viollet-le-Duc.

EN CHAMPAGNE

69. Reims, 1665.

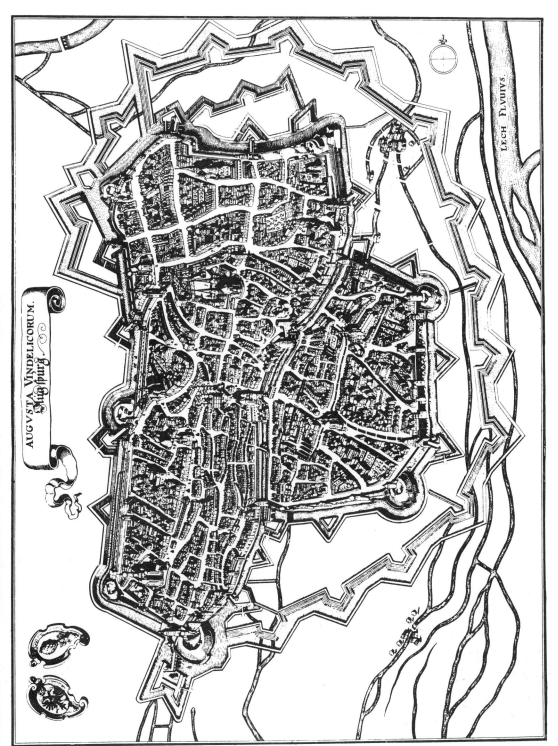

AUGVSTA VINDELICORUM.
Augspurg

LECH FLVVIVS

70. Augsburg, 1643.

71. Lucca, airview from northeast.

72. Lucca, flanked curtain,
    northwest front.

73. Lucca, bastion, south front.

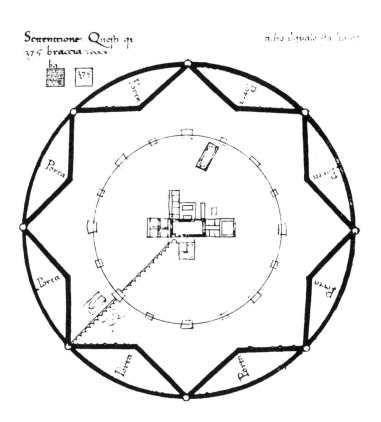

74. Lucca, glacis with lunette, north front.

75. Antonio Filarete, plan of an ideal city (Sforzinda), 1464.

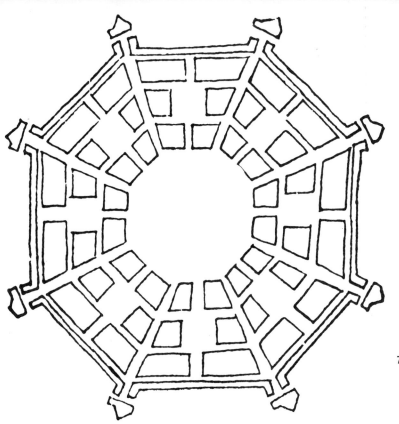

76. Francesco di Giorgio Martini, ideal city plans from the *Codex Magliabecchianus.*

77. Villefranche-sur-Meuse, 1544, Girolamo Marini.

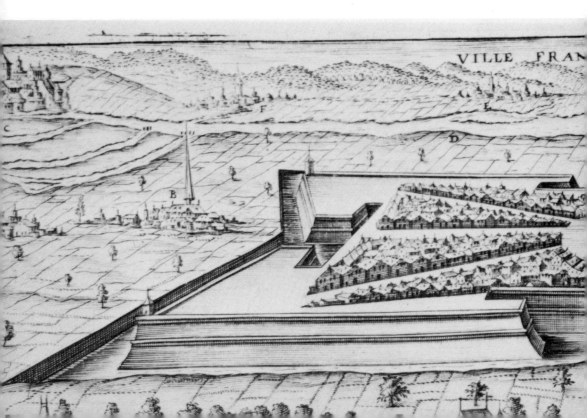

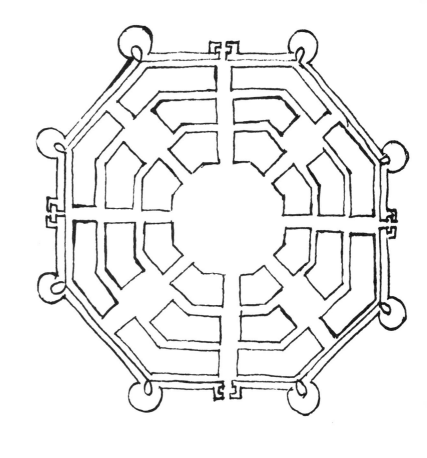

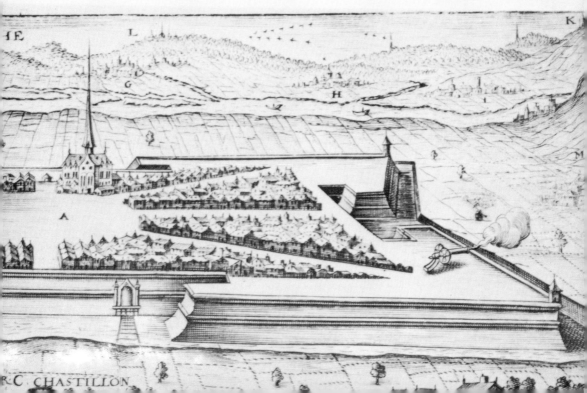

PHILIP   PE VILLE

PHILIP⸗
POPOLIS
vulgo Phi⸗
lippeuillę
munitiß:
Comitat⸗
Hanno⸗
niæ Opp:

78. Philippeville, 1555, Sebastian van Noyen.

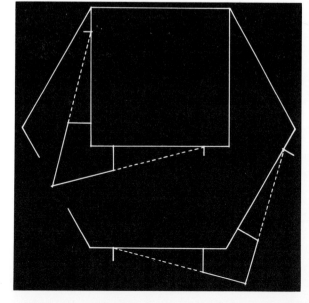

79. Comparison of bastions drawn for a
    square and a hexagon with equal sides.

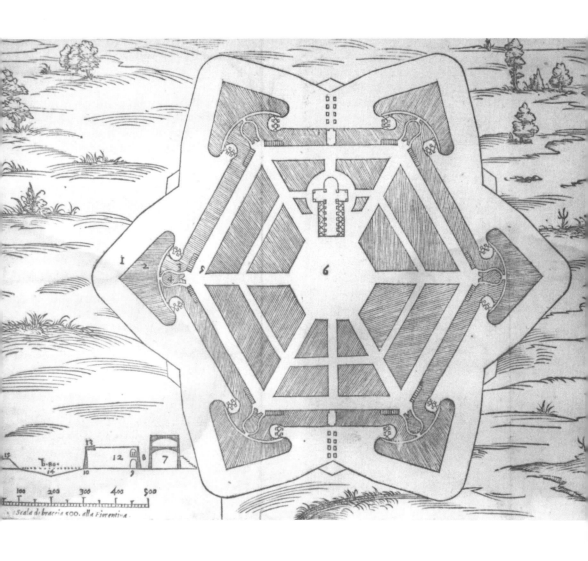

80. Antonio Lupicini, ideal city, 1582.

81. Palmanova, airview.

82. Palmanova, bastion, ditch, and Porta Aquilaea, 1593.

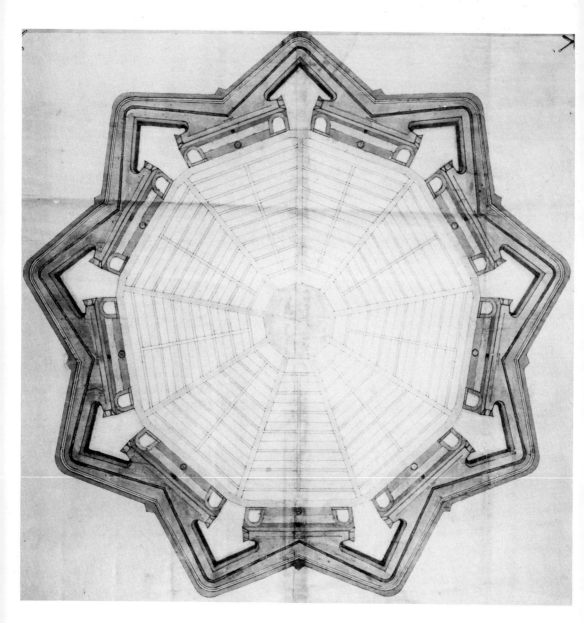

83. Plan for Palmanova project, 1593, anonymous.

84. Plan for Palmanova project, 1593, anonymous.

85. Palmanova as built, plan by Cacogliatti, c. 1695.

86. Plan of Palmanova, 1851.

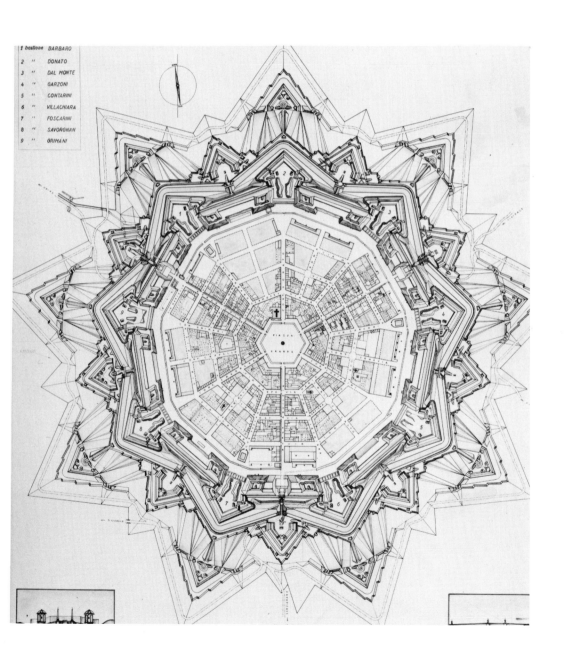

1 bastione BARBARO
2   "   DONATO
3   "   DAL MONTE
4   "   GARZONI
5   "   CONTARINI
6   "   VILLACHIARA
7   "   FOSCARINI
8   "   SAVORGNAN
9   "   GRIMANI

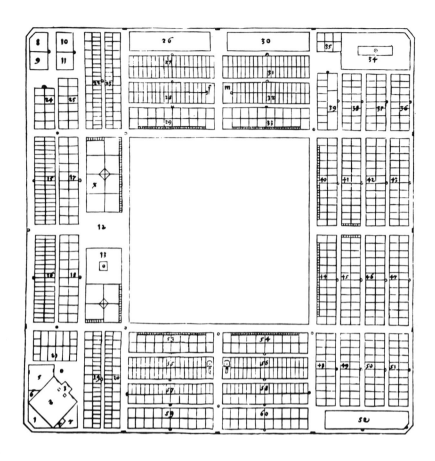

87. Albrecht Dürer, plan of an ideal city, 1520's.

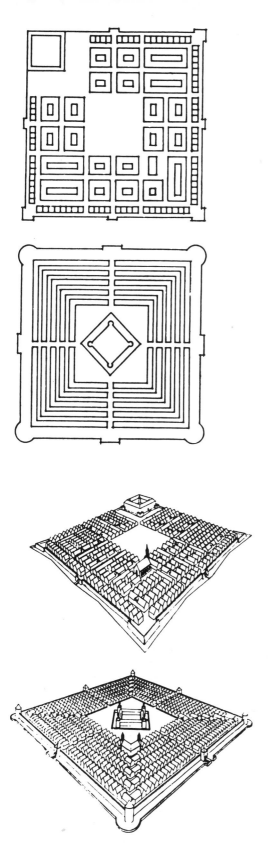

88. Heinrich Schickhardt, designs for Freudenstadt, 1596, perspective reconstructions of two of several designs for the project.

89. Neuf-Brisach, 1699, Vauban.

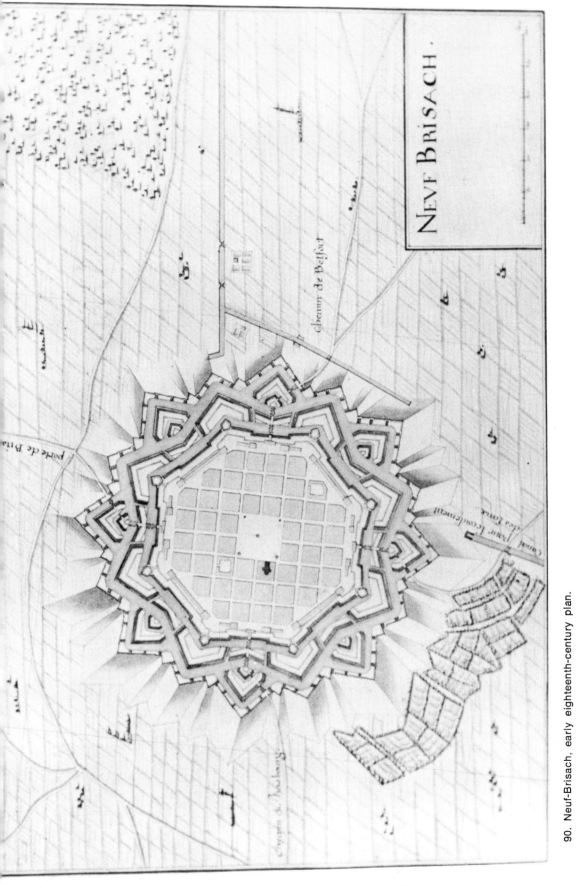

NEVF BRISACH.

Chemin de Belfort

porte de Bri

Canal pour Lecoulement des Eaux

chemin de Strasbourg

90. Neuf-Brisach, early eighteenth-century plan.

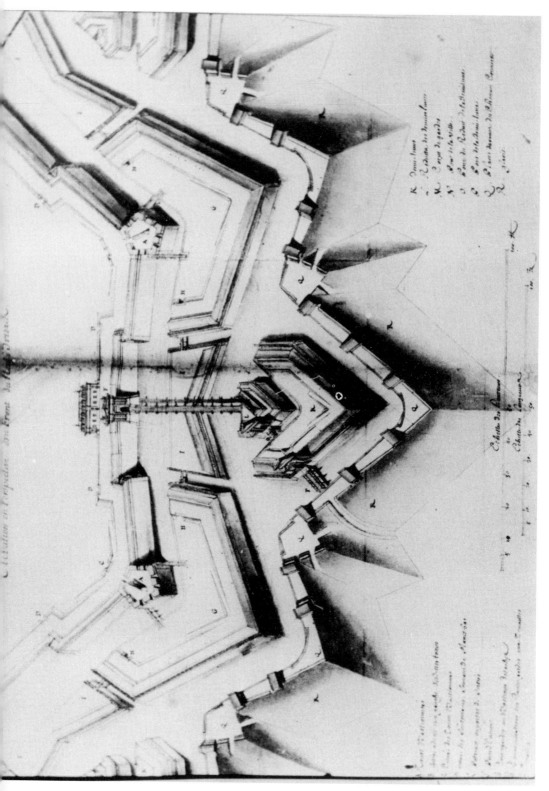

91. Perspective view of a Neuf-Brisach front, early eighteenth-century drawing, anonymous.

NOTES

1. Human geographers have made a typological distinction between nucleated "stone cities" and open "green cities." This volume is concerned essentially with the former, since the latter, as the term implies, generally were not surrounded with continuous walls, *i.e.*, they were not fortified (*cf.* Conrad Arensberg, "The Urban in Cross Cultural Perspective," in Elizabeth Eddy [ed.], *Urban Anthropology,* Proceedings of the Southern Anthropological Association, University of Georgia, 1968. I am indebted to Prof. George Collins for this reference).

2. Lewis Mumford, *The City in History*, New York, 1961, chapters 1 and 2.

3. Mumford feels that the farmers forgot how to use arms and, consequently, were no longer able to defend themselves. But it is a little difficult to see how, at this primitive stage of weaponry, the swinging of the battle axe would have differed markedly from the handling of the equally lethal woodsman's axe. In any case, it seems likely that, during this transitional stage, the farmers did most of their own hunting.

4. Armin von Gerkan, *Griechische Staedteanlagen*, Berlin-Leipzig, 1924.

5. Kathleen Kenyon, *Digging up Jericho*, London, 1957.

6. James Mellaart, *Çatal Hüyük: a Neolithic Town in Anatolia*, London, 1967, gives a crisp and lucid account of the fascinating finds made at the site.

7. James Mellaart, *Earliest Civilizations of the Near East*, London, 1965, pp. 102–113.

8. Leo Oppenheim, *Ancient Mesopotamia*, Chicago, 1964, p. 128.

9. For a summary of ancient siege methods and the defenses they had to overcome, see Heinz Waschow, *4000 Jahre Kampf um die Mauer*, Bottrop, 1938.

10. Henry Frankfort, *The Art and Architecture of the Ancient Orient*, London, 1954, p. 169, dates Zincirli to the late second millennium B.C.; Oppenheim, *Ancient Mesopotamia*, to the eighth century B.C.

11. *Ibid.*, pp. 73–76.

12. Oppenheim, *Ancient Mesopotamia*; p. 134, connects this Assyrian arrangement with that of the private house in Mesopotamia, where living quarters were placed as far as possible from the street.

13. Frankfort feels that the Assyrian builders aimed for symmetry and explains all irregularities as results of poor surveying methods. This is a little difficult to accept in view of the excellent results achieved by the Egyptians some two thousand years earlier. Either the town and palace were built in too great a hurry to allow for accuracy in their layout, or the Assyrians were not as concerned with symmetry as Frankfort believes.

14. Frankfort has suggested that the Egyptian civilization never developed a truly urban character, like that of Mesopotamia, but remained essentially rural. In addition to the cultural, social political, and religious factors that have been cited to explain this fact, one that has been overlooked so far, but which might well deserve some attention, is the lack of urban fortifications. Without enceintes Egyptian cities lacked concentration and definition; they gradually melted into the surrounding landscape and people living near the periphery may never really have known whether they were rural or urban residents.

15. On the bottom of the front side of the Palette of Narmer, the King, symbolized by a bull, is shown destroying an enemy town that is represented in the form of a circular, tower-studded wall. (Paul Lampl, *Cities and Planning in the Ancient Near East*, New York, 1968, *Fig. 2*).

16. Alexander Badawy, *A History of Egyptian Architecture*, Berkeley, 1966, p. 229. It is difficult to get a clear picture of an Egyptian glacis from Badawy's description. A true glacis is an artificial slope that falls outward and away from the outer rim of the ditch; it was intended to improve the defenders' field of vision and, in antiquity, to impede the movement of heavy siege machinery. In antiquity and the Middle Ages a glacis was never very wide and its effectiveness was limited. After the advent of firearms, however, and then for somewhat different reasons, it be-

comes an extremely important and integral part of all fortifications (see below, p. 124).

17. The question of priority remains unresolved at this point. Current scholarship seems to favor Mesopotamia as the source of many Egyptian cultural and technical developments.

18. The manner in which the Tiryns' walls and buildings are fused into a cohesive unit is reminiscent of Hacilar. In fact, while most of the traffic at Tiryns moved at ground level, access to parts of the walls must have been across rooftops.

19. Von Gerkan, p. 7.

20. It is generally assumed that some kind of settlement must have stood at the foot of the citadel hill, although no evidence of it seems to have been found so far.

21. It is most tempting to associate the new concept of aggressive defense with the invention of the catapult. A new weapon which could do serious damage to the defenses and even threaten the civilian population inside the town from a distance that was beyond the effective range of the defending archers might well have impelled a drastic revision of defensive strategy. The near-contemporaneity of the two developments, however, raises problems.
Ancient hurling devices used two principles of propulsion: tension (the bending of a bow or heavy plank) and torsion (the twisting of heavy elastic cords or fibers). It is believed that the tension catapult was invented either by the Carthaginians or the Syracusans around 400 B.C. and that the first torsion catapults appeared in the siege trains of Alexander the Great (A. R. Hall, "Military Technology," in C. Singer and others, *A History of Technology*, Oxford, 1956, vol. II, pp. 699–770).
Dionysius the Elder of Syracuse reputedly was the first Greek to use tension catapults. He also was the first to design fortifications in accordance with the novel concept of a mobile and active defense. Could he have been far-sighted enough to appreciate fully the potential of a brand-new, and supposedly untested, weapon to revolutionize age-old defensive concepts? In their earliest stages of development catapults could not have been very effective. Perhaps an earlier date for the invention of the catapult than the generally accepted one should be inferred from the known building dates of the fortifications at Syracuse and Selinus. Unless we accept the unlikely notion of an accidental contemporaneity, the structures at Syracuse and Selinus suggest that the catapult and its effects were well known around 400 B.C. and that we should think of it as an invention of the fifth, rather than the fourth century B.C.

22. The pertinent topographical and technical studies of the Castel Euryelos are found in F. S. Cavallari and A. Holm, *Topografia archeologica di Siracusa*, Palermo, 1883, and L. Mauceri, *Il castello Euriala nella storia e nell'arte*, Rome, 1928. For a military analysis, see E. Rocchi, *Fonti storiche dell'architettura militare*, Rome, 1908, pp. 37–44.

23. The purpose of these towers has never been fully explained. They seem to be the last structures to be built at the site and may well have served as catapult platforms. If they were interconnected, as shown in the reconstruction (*Fig.* 17), they would have provided the defenders with a spacious platform on which to maneuver their engines. The estimated original height of these towers of 15 meters would have given the defenders a range advantage over the enemy. Since the range of catapults toward the end of the century is said to have been close to 200 meters with missiles weighing up to 80 kilograms, (c. 180 lbs.), (Rocchi, *Fonti storiche*, p. 22), both the outer ditch and the main gateway could have been adequately covered from the towers.

24. J. Hulot and G. Fougères, *Sélinonte: la ville, l'acropole et ses temples*, Paris, 1910.

25. Armin von Gerkan, "Die Stadtmauern," *Milet*, II, 3, Berlin-Leipzig, 1935.

26. Later modifications did not alter the wall's basic design. The installation of drawbridges between wall sections permitted the isolation of individual units from the rest of the wall; at the same time, they improved lateral communication and facilitated the movement of heavy defense weapons.

27. Von Gerkan's plan of Veii may not be too accurate, and it is shown here only to illustrate the meandering path of Etruscan wall circuits as they followed the edges of a plateau. Veii was destroyed by the Romans in 395 B.C. after a ten-year siege, and the indicated street plan may reflect later Roman occupancy of the site. Also, towers were not a standard feature of Etruscan fortifications.

28. Perhaps the statement that these rites were taken over from the Etruscans should not be taken too literally. It is a little difficult to see how the Etruscans performed the *limitatio* on the sites which they generally chose for their cities. Running a plow along the edges of a cliff not only would have been difficult, but purposeless. The *inauguratio* and the *consecratio* may well have been genuine Etruscan practices, but the intermediate two steps could just as well have been added by the Romans themselves, who then sanctified them with a fabricated tradition. For an extended discussion of the meaning of these practices, see Joseph Rykwert, "The Idea of a Town," *Forum*, No. 3 (Amsterdam, 1963).

29. Frank E. Brown, *Cosa I: History and Topography*, Rome, 1951. The wall around the consecrated area of the arx in the town's south corner may at first create the impression that Cosa was a citadel city. In fact, however, this wall had no military purpose and its significance was purely symbolic. It also served as a retaining wall and may have had the aesthetic function of providing the capitolium with an imposing socle. The towers on the western side were added during the Middle Ages.

30. The first-known complete and systematic towered fortification system in central Italy is the ashlar tufa wall of Falerii Novi which was built around 241 B.C.

31. The generic term "castrum plan" seems to imply that the plan was derived from that of the Roman army encampment (*castrum*). It should be mentioned that there has never been, nor is there now, general agreement on this point. According to Frontinus (IV, 1–14) the Romans developed the *castrum* form only after 275 B.C., when they defeated Pyrrhus at Beneventum and took note of the layout and fortification of the Greek commander's field camp. However, Ostia, a Roman maritime colony with a *castrum* plan, had already been founded in 330 B.C., and Polybius (VI, 31–41) states flatly that the form of Roman army encampments was derived from city plans. The problem is discussed at some length in Axel Boethius, *The Golden House of Nero*, Ann Arbor, 1960, pp. 42 ff.

32. The generally square form of the Roman castrum was not without its critics. Vitruvius (I:V.2) specifically writes that the plan of a city should not be square, but round or polygonal. Advocates of the square plan, however, contended that circles and polygons were too easily surrounded and that square shapes impelled besiegers to spread out their forces more thinly.

33. Archeological purists refer to the Aurelian wall as medieval rather than late classical; the distinction is meaningless since medieval military architecture did not introduce any significant changes into Roman fortification methods until the twelfth century.

34. Of 87 investigated Italian towns, only 17 turned out to be medieval foundations; all others stand on ancient sites (Ernst Egli, *Geschichte des Staedtebaus*, Zurich, 1959–67, vol. 2, p. 32).

35. Rocchi (*Fonti storiche*, p. 59) states that 60,000 (!) castles were built in France during the Middle Ages, but does not give the source of his information.

36. The medieval citizen's esteem for city walls is summarized in W. Braunfels, *Mittelalterliche Stadtbaukunst in der Toskana*, Berlin, 1953, pp. 45 ff. Among other interesting references to the town wall's significance, he points out that pictures of Paradise often show it surrounded by a merlated wall; that in Expulsion scenes Adam and Eve are always driven out of Eden through a gate; and that in Giotto's allegories in the Arena Chapel in Padua, Justice is shown inside a city, while Injustice is represented outside a city gate.

37. The only new siege engine to appear during the Middle Ages was the trebuchet, or counter-poise catapult, which flung its missiles from the long arm of a pivoted spar that was activated by heavy weights attached to its short arm; its advantage was that it did not have to rely upon the short-lived elasticity of

the cords that operated the torsion catapult. The first trebuchets made their appearance in Europe around 1200 A.D. and the question whether they are a European invention or were brought back from the Near East by the crusaders remains unsettled (P. E. Cleator, *Weapons of War*, New York, 1968; also Rocchi, *Fonti storiche*, pp. 222–224).

38. Viollet-le-Duc, *La cité de Carcassone*, Paris, n.d. In addition to the surviving Roman monuments, of course, medieval planners also had the guidance of classical military writers, such as Caesar and Flavius Vegetius Renatus, whose works were widely read and often copied during the Middle Ages. The popularity of Vegetius is amply attested by the great number of copies that were made of his *Epitoma rei militaris*. Over 150 of these copies, dating from the tenth to the fifteenth centuries, are said to be still in existence (Max Jaehns, *Geschichte der Kriegswissenschaften*, Munich, 1889, vol. 1, p. 120).

39. Any visitor to Montagnana who is interested in the town's history and the design of its walls will find a most knowledgeable and cooperative guide in Ing Stanislao Carazzolo, founder of the Centro Studi sui Castelli, a small but select library on military architecture, located in the Palazzo Communale.

40. Most medieval towers had open backs, a design that was both economical and practical; it reduced construction costs and, at the same time, greatly simplified the logistics of furnishing the towers' different levels with heavy ordnance.

41. While the composition of gun powder may have been known in Europe as early as the eighth century, one of the first authenticated uses of cannon took place in 1331, when the German Barons von Spielemberg and von Kreuzberg attacked Cividale in Friulia (H. Delbrueck, *Geschichte der Kriegskunst*, Berlin, 1920, IV, pp. 29 ff.).

42. It was argued that slanting surfaces would cause cannonballs to glance off rather than shatter them. Strong battering of the lower parts of walls had been tried occasionally during the Middle Ages, but never found general acceptance. On one hand, it facilitated escalade and, on the other, it decreased the effectiveness of machicoulis defenses, since the base of the wall was moved forward and out of their vertical range.

43. No documentary proof for the attribution of San Leo to Francesco di Giorgio has been found so far. But the forms of curtain and towers are so characteristic of the Sienese architect's style that they allow little doubt of his authorship. One can compare the numerous fortification designs in his extremely important and influential treatise, published by Cesare Saluzzo and Carlo Promis as: *Trattato di architettura civile e militare di Francesco di Giorgio Martini*, Turin, 1841. A new edition that correlates several copies of two versions of Francesco's treatise, and contains reduced facsimiles of most of his designs, was published recently by Corrado Maltese (Francesco di Giorgio Martini, *Trattati di architettura, ingeneria e arte militare*, Milan, 1967).

44. Pontelli himself must have realized that machicoulis galleries were obsolete at his time, as most of the arcades at Ostia are blind; only every third one has an open bottom. Nevertheless, their use persists into the sixteenth century. And then, rather than abandoning completely a feature which had been visually associated with military architecture for centuries, architects replaced them with bracket-supported cornices before finally discarding them (Nettuno, *Fig. 63*, built in 1501–1502, and Peruzzi's Baluardo Pispini at Siena, *Fig. 64*, built about 1528).

In this connection, it might be worth some while to investigate a possible link between military machicolations and the emphasis which Renaissance architects placed upon the crowning cornices of their civil structures.

45. The large, square openings below the cordone are not embrasures, but ventilation shafts leading to the casemates below. Embrasures can be seen on the far left of the structure, at the very base of the mastio's polygonal foot.

46. This was the first occasion on which iron cannonballs were used on a large scale. Other innovations introduced by the French at this time included the mounting of guns on permanent carriages and the use of horses, instead of oxen, as draught animals. The effectiveness of French artillery was such that many

Neapolitan garrisons surrendered at the mere threat of a bombardment (F. L. Taylor, *The Art of War in Italy, 1494–1529*, Cambridge, 1921).

47. Francesco di Giorgio was one of the first to realize this fact; in his *Trattato* (V, 3) ca. 1485, he writes that "the ancients did not know our artillery," implying that, as far as fortification is concerned, nothing can be learned from them.

48. Michelangelo was a strong advocate of earthen fortifications and used them at Florence in 1529. Treatises expounding the virtues of tamped earth construction were written by G. B. della Valle di Venafro (1521), G. B. Bellucci (1545), Giacomo Lanteri (1559), and others (H. de la Croix, "The Literature on Fortification in Renaissance Italy," *Technology and Culture*, IV, 1, Winter 1963).

In connection with subsequent passages in the text, it may be argued that there is no significant difference between earth works with masonry shirts on the one hand, and masonry walls backed up by earthen terraces on the other. The contention here is that two basically different concepts are involved. In the former case, the builder thinks in terms of stamped earth constructions with reinforcing timbers which may or may not be provided with masonry shirts to prevent erosion; in the latter case, he thinks in terms of solid and massive masonry walls, complete with interior buttresses, vaults, and so on, which may or may not be backed up by earthen terraces. The observation that masonry, when crumbling under bombardment, tended to fall outward to create a rough ramp for the final assault (cf. N. Macchiavelli, *Dell'arte della guerra*, Book VII) made it particularly important for advocates of solid masonry construction to devise a method for protecting the breach.

49. Lodovico Marinelli, "Fra Giocondo, 1435–1515," *Rivista d'artiglieria*, Vol. II, 1902.

50. Although kept busy at Treviso, Fra Giocondo was frequently called to Padua for advice on the refortification of that city, which had been lost to the League in June 1509, but was reoccupied by the Venetians a month later. His recommendations there were just as radical as those he had given for Treviso, but met with less public resistance probably because the town had already been sacked once. The buildings along the town's periphery were razed and, within three months, the six-mile-long medieval enceinte was modernized in accordance with the friar's specifications. Here the artillery platforms were mined so that they could be blown up if they fell into the enemy's hands.

By September 1509 Padua's defenses were in good enough condition to withstand an Imperial siege. Attacks were concentrated on the "Bastione della gatta." When it appeared that it could no longer be held, the defenders withdrew from the bastion and blew it up, with a resultant loss to the enemy of over 200 men. Shortly after this disaster the siege was lifted (Giacomo Rusconi, *Le mura di Padova*, Padua, 1905).

Padua's fortifications underwent numerous modifications in later years and only here and there some remnants survive that reflect their 1509 appearance (*Fig. 57*).

51. E. Rocchi (*Fonti storiche*, pp. 260–262) attributes the fort to Antonio da Sangallo the Elder. P. A. Guglielmotti (*Storia delle fortificazioni nella spiaggia romana*, Rome, 1880) suggests that Antonio may have used one of the designs from Giuliano's *Taccuino Senese*, although most of the fortification designs in this work seem to date after 1501. If Rocchi (*op. cit.*, p. 258) feels that Antonio had Giuliano's help when he designed the fort at Civita Castellana, then the revolutionary solution of Nettuno seems to make such cooperation even more likely, especially since Giuliano is generally considered to have been the more imaginative of the two brothers.

52. Precedence has been claimed for the enceinte of Urbino which was begun in 1513 by Francesco Maria I della Rovere, heir of the Montefeltri, in anticipation of the aggression of Pope Leo X who wanted to secure the duchy for one of his Medici relatives. However, work on the enceinte had not progressed very far (and what had been built was torn down later) when Francesco Maria was forced to renounce his duchy. The present enceinte was built after 1521, when the duke reestablished himself at Urbino. There is no certainty that he used his 1513 designs for this enceinte (L. Celli, "Le fortificazioni di Urbino. . . ," *Nuova rivista misena*, VIII, 1895, pp. 5–10).

53. Similarly historicizing enceintes are found at Padua and Verona; the latter is particularly interesting, as it contains elements that reach all the way from the Middle Ages down to the nineteenth century.

54. Giovanni Sforza, *L'ingegnere Jacopo Seghizzi, detto il Frate da Modena,* Lucca, 1886. Although the construction of the Lucca fortifications was not completed until the early seventeenth century, and although numerous other military architects had supervision of the work at one time or another, the project was carried out pretty much according to Paciotto's original plans.

55. Lucca's fortifications are also among the best preserved in Europe, thanks to the foresight of a nineteenth century city council which, when most other enceintes were ruthlessly torn down or built over, decided to convert Lucca's into a public park; it is now one of the world's great promenades.

56. Francesco de Marchi, *Della architettura militare*, Brescia, 1599, III–147. This treatise is one of the most complete summaries not only of 16th century theories of fortification, but also of the century's general urban ideals. Completed around 1565 and published posthumously, the 1599 edition is extremely rare. It is republished by Luigi Marini as *Trattato d'architettura militare di Francesco de Marchi*, Rome, 1810.

57. H. de la Croix, "Military Architecture and the Radial City Plan in Sixteenth Century Italy," *The Art Bulletin*, XII-4, (December, 1960).

58. Antonio Lupicini, *Architettura militare, libro primo*, (Florence, 1582), caption I, p. 15.

59. H. de la Croix, "Palmanova: A Study in Sixteenth Century Urbanism," *Saggi e memorie di storia dell'arte*, Vol. 5 (Florence, 1967).

60. Bonaiuto Lorini, *Della fortificazione libri* V, Venice, 1597, I-20, pp. 54–55.

61. Vincenzo Scamozzi, *Dell'idea della architettura universale*, Venice 1615, II-29, pp. 206–207.

62. The attempt was unsuccessful on all counts. Palmanova failed to develop into the flourishing urban center which its civilian planners had envisioned; planned for a population of 20,000, it never attracted more than 5,000 people. And its urban picture was not greatly improved by the change in the design of its enormous central piazza; due to its size (its diameter from corner to corner exceeds 175 meters) it looks like an open field and cannot be appreciated as an urban unit, no matter what its boundaries. Aside from its fascinating plan and impressive fortifications, Palmanova has remained a rather dull garrison town.

63. Note that the features of the plan lend themselves to varying interpretations. The ditch, for instance, can be read either as a very wide single, or as a double ditch. In the latter case, we would be looking at a double enceinte, instead of a single one with outworks. This and other ambiguities in the arrangement of traditional fortificatory elements suggest that their functions also have been altered. At Neuf-Brisach, in fact, the outworks have become emancipated and their formerly auxiliary function has become a primary one.

64. The glacis is one of Palmanova's greatest assets, as it is the only one known to me that has been almost completely preserved. Unfortunately it is in the process of being destroyed by NATO (?) forces who are using it as training grounds for tanks and armored vehicles. Needless to say that the delicately landscaped and contoured terrain is rapidly being leveled and plowed under.

65. Other contributions which Brialmont made to the science of modern fortification include the use of armor to protect guns and the design of turrets with retractable cannon. Although Liège, Namur, and Antwerp were reduced in short order by the German armies at the beginning of World War I, the similarly fortified Verdun in France was able, albeit at tremendous cost, to withstand even the heaviest assaults the Germans could mount against it. While the fall of the Belgian fortresses must have been a severe shock to military architects, the success of Verdun seems to have maintained their faith in fixed, permanent fortifications sufficiently that the construction of the Maginot and Siegfried lines did not seem like folly to them.

GLOSSARY

BALLISTA. Ancient hurling device (in the form of a large crossbow?); ancient usage apparently made no clear distinction between ballista and catapult (*see below*); most frequently the distinction appears to have been based upon different types of ammunition used, i.e., the ballista shot arrows, while the catapult hurled rocks.

BARBICAN. A medieval fortified outwork; detached from inner ring of fortifications and frequently placed in front of gates.

BASTIDES. Fortified towns founded in south-west France during twelfth and thirteenth centuries.

BASTION. A gun platform projecting from fortress walls, consisting of two flanks (*see below*) behind a triangular head formed by two faces terminating in a salient angle.

BREASTWORKS. *See* Parapet.

CASEMENT. Bomb-proof chamber, usually of masonry, from which cannon can shoot through embrasures (*see below*).

CASTELLO. *See* Rocca.

CATAPULT. Mechanical hurling device, using either tension, torsion, or counter-poise for the propulsion of missiles.

CIRCUMVALLATION. Walls or ramparts surrounding an open or inhabited area.

CORDONE. A stringcourse, usually of masonry, from which cannon can shoot through embrasures (*see below*).

COUNTERSCARP. Outer rim of ditch; slope of walls from bottom to outer rim of ditch (*see* escarp *below*).

COVERED WAY. A path along the rim of the counterscarp, protected from the glacis by a shoulder-high parapet.

CRENELLATION. Toothlike breastworks on wall tops, formed by alternating embrasures and merlons.

CROWNWORKS. Crown-shaped outworks.

CURTAIN. Stretch of wall connecting the towers or bastions of a fortified front.

EMBRASURE. Slit or opening in parapet or wall through which defenders can shoot.

ENCEINTE. A fortified enclosure.

ENFILADE. To rake with gunfire; to shoot in the direction of the length of a trench or line of troops.

ESCALADE. To mount the ramparts of a fortress by means of ladders; from Latin *scala*—ladder.

ESCARP (SCARP). Slope of inner ditch walls and of outer surfaces of curtains and bastions.

FLANK. Side of bastion which immediately adjoins the curtain.

GLACIS. Artificial slope downward and outward from the rim of the counterscarp (*see* note 16).

HORNWORKS. Horn-shaped outworks.

KEEP. Large tower in medieval strongholds, serving as living quarters and last refuge.

LIMES. Originally a term meaning "boundary" and used by Latin writers to denote "marked frontiers." Term was expanded by modern historians to describe the frontiers of the Roman Empire generally, and its permanently fortified sections specifically; thus, Hadrian's Wall in northern England (*Limes Britannicus*), and the fortified line between the Rhine and Danube rivers (*Limes Germanicus*).

LUNETTE. Detached outwork placed outside ditch and in front of a bastion; usually consists of two faces forming a salient angle.

MACHICOLATION. Opening in the floor of a gallery projecting outward from walltop (machicoulis gallery); designed for the vertical defense of walls and towers from above; derived from French *macher*, to crush.

MAGISTRAL LINE. Main line of fortified defenses.

MASTIO. Italian word for keep (*see above*).

MERLONS. Solid sections of a crenellated parapet; they flank embrasures.

ORILLION. Shoulderlike projection of bastion, designed to protect the flank.

OUTWORKS. Any fortifications outside the magistral line; often named after the appearance of their plans (e.g. *tenaille*—pincers; *demi-lune* —half moon, and so forth).

PARAPET. Breastworks atop walls and bastions, designed to protect defenders from enemy fire.

POLIORCETICS. The science of siege warfare; from the Greek *poliorketes* —taker of cities.

POLIS. Greek term for a city as a political unit.

POMOERIUM. A streetlike open area running parallel with and adjacent to the interior base of the walls.

POSTERN. Gate for sorties; from Latin *postera*—back door.

RAMPARTS. A defense or protective barrier.

RAVELIN. Detached outwork, generally shaped like a lunette, but placed in front of a curtain.

RETIRATA. Temporary earthen rampart, built behind the main wall to seal off a breach.

REVETMENT. Facing of stone (or some other material) to sustain an embankment.

ROCCA. Italian term for a fortress that serves primarily a military purpose; as opposed to *castello*, which generally means a fortified residence.

SAP(PING). Originally to undermine; to dig a trench or gallery from the attacker's line to a point beneath the defender's works for the purpose of either destroying them or of gaining entry into the stronghold.

TENAILLE. *See* Outworks, *above*.

TERRACE. All earthworks built up above the natural ground level.

TREBUCHET. Counterpoise catapult (*see* note 37).

BIBLIOGRAPHY

Since the literature on city planning is better known and more readily accessible than that on military history and fortification, this bibliography is intended to acquaint the reader with a few of the key works in the latter field only. Some general works on city planning, excavation reports, and histories of individual cities relevant to the text are listed in the Notes and are not repeated. The bibliography is divided into two parts, the first listing works that were written before 1800, the second those that appeared after that date. For a more complete listing of titles, especially of Renaissance *Trattati*, the reader is referred to: H. de la Croix, "The Literature on Fortification in Renaissance Italy," *Technology and Culture*, Vol. IV, No. 1, Winter 1963.

Literature before 1800 (printed works only):

Alghisi, Galasso. *Delle fortificazione libri tre.* Venice, 1570.

Busca, Gabriello. *Della architettura militare. . . .* Milan, 1601.

Bellucci, Giovan Battista. *Nuova invenzione di fabricar fortezze.* Venice, 1598 (written *ca.* 1550).

Cataneo, Girolamo. *Opera nuova di fortificare. . . .* Brescia, 1564.

Cataneo, Pietro. *I quattro primi libri di architettura.* Venice, 1554.

Caesar, C. Julius. *The Gallic War.* Translated by H. J. Edwards, Cambridge, 1952 (written in first century B.C.).

(da Pizzano, Christina). *Les faicts d'armes et de chevalerie.* Paris, 1488 (written ca. 1410). Published without author's name; translated by W. Caxton and published as *A Book of Christine of Pyse Drawn Out of Vegetius De Re Militari*, Westminster, 1489.

de Marchi, Francesco. *Della architettura militare.* Brescia, 1599 (written *ca.* 1565; republished by Luigi Marini, Rome, 1810).

di Giorgio Martini, Francesco. *Trattato dell'architettura civile e militare.* Turin, 1841 (written *ca.* 1485; new edition by Corrado Maltese, Milan, 1967).

Doegens, M. *Heutiges Tages uebliche Kriegsbaukunst.* Amsterdam, 1648.

Dürer, Albrecht. *Etliche Unterricht zur Befestigung der Stett, Schloss und Flecken*, Nuremberg, 1527. Reprinted with introduction and notes by Martin Biddle, Westmead, England, 1970.

Errard, J. *Traitée de la fortification.* Paris, 1601.

Faeschen, J. R. *Des befestigten Europae erste Centuria,* Nuremberg, 1727.

Floriani, Pietro Paolo. *Difesa et offesa della piazze.* Macerata, 1630.

Lanteri, Jacomo. *Due libri del modo di fare le fortificazione di terra.* Venice, 1559.

Lorini, Bonaiuto. *Delle fortificatione libri V.* Venice, 1597.

Lupicini, Antonio. *Architettura militare libro primo.* Florence, 1582.

Macchiavelli, Niccolò. *Dell'arte della guerra libri VII.* Florence, 1521.

Maggi, Girolamo and Castriotto, Fusto. *Della fortificatione delle città libri tre.* Venice, 1564.

Mora, Domenico. *Tre quesiti in dialogo sopra il fare batterie, fortificare una città et. . . .* Venice, 1567.

Perret, Jacques. *Des fortifications et artifices d'architecture et perspective.* Paris, 1597.

Sardi, Pietro. *La corona imperiale dell'architettura militare.* Venice, 1618.

Scamozzi, Vincenzo. *Dell'idea dell'architettura universale.* Venice, 1615.

Speckle, D. *Architectura von Festungen.* Strassburg, 1589.

Tartaglia, Nicola. *Sul modo di fortificare le città rispetto la forma.* Venice, 1536.

Tensini, Francesco. *La fortificazione, guardia, difesa et espugnazione delle fortezze.* Venice, 1623.

Valle di Venafro, G. B. della. *Vallo libro contenente appertinentie ad capitani, retenere et fortificare una città con bastioni. . . .* Venice, 1524.

Valturio, Roberto. *De re militari.* Verona, 1472.

Vauban, S. le Prestre de. *Traité des sièges et de l'attaque des places,* Paris, 1795 (a recent English edition appeared under the title: *A Manual of Siegecraft and Fortification*, Ann Arbor, 1968).

Vegetius, Renatus Flavius. *Epitomae Rei Militaris.* Stuttgart, 1967 (written in fourth century A.D.).

Vitruvius, Pollio. *Ten Books on Architecture.* Translated by M. H. Morgan, Cambridge, 1914 (written in first century A.D.).

Zanchi, Giovan Battista. *Del modo di fortificar le citta.* Venice, 1554.

Literature after 1800:

Adcock, F. E. *The Roman Art of War under the Republic.* Cambridge, 1940.

————. *The Greek and Macedonian Art of War.* Berkeley-Los Angeles, 1957.

Cleator, P. E. *Weapons of War.* New York, 1968.

Daniels, E. *Geschichte des Kriegswesens.* Leipzig, 1910.

D'Ayala, M. *Dell'arte militare in Italia.* Florence, 1851.

Delaborde, F. *L'expédition de Charles VIII en Italie.* Paris, 1888.

de la Croix, H. "Military Architecture and the Radial City Plan in 16th Century Italy," *The Art Bulletin*, XLII, No. 4. December, 1960.

Delbrueck, H. *Geschichte der Kriegskunst.* Berlin, 1920.

Ebhard, Bodo von. *Der Wehrbau Europas im Mittelalter.* Berlin, 1939.

Guglielmotti, P. A. *Storia delle fortificazioni nella spiaggia Romana.* Rome, 1880.

Jaehns, M. *Geschichte der Kriegswissenschaften.* Munich, 1889.

Hall, A. R. "Military Technology," in Singer, C., *et al, A History of Technology.* Oxford, 1956.

Maggiorotti, L. A. *Architetti e architettura militare.* Rome, 1933–1939.

Montross, L. *War through the Ages.* New York, 1960.

Oman, C. *A History of the Art of War: the Middle Ages . . .* London, 1905.

O'Neill, B. H. St. J. *Castles and Cannons: A Study of Early Artillery Fortification in England*, Oxford, 1960.

Promis, C. "Biografie . . . ," in *Miscellanea di storia italiana,* Vols. I, 1862; IV, 1863; XII, 1871; XIV, 1874.

Rocchi, E. *Le origini della fortificazione moderna.* Rome, 1894.

————. *Le fonti storiche dell'architettura militare.* Rome, 1908.

Schmitthenner, P. *Krieg und Kriegfuehrung im Wandel der Weltgeschichte.* Potsdam, 1930.

Schuchardt, C. *Die Burg im Wandel der Weltgeschichte.* Potsdam, 1931.

Taylor, F. L. *The Art of War in Italy, 1494–1529.* Cambridge, 1921.

Viollet-le-Duc. *Histoire d'une Fortresse.* Paris, 1874.

Viollet-le-Duc., E. *Essai sur l'histoire de l'architecture militaire dans le moyen-âge*. Paris, 1854.

Waschow, H. *4000 Jahre Kampf um die Mauer*. Leipzig, 1938.

Wauvermans, H. *L'architecture militaire flamande et italienne au XVIe siècle*. Liège, 1877.

INDEX

SOURCES OF ILLUSTRATIONS

Alinari, Florence, 32.

Alexander Badawy. *A History of Egyptian Architecture*, 9, 10.

Courtesy of Barenreiter Verlag, Wilhelmshohe, 70.

Biblioteca Marciana, Venice, 56, 83, 84.

Braun and Hogenberg. *Civitates Orbis Terrarum,* 78.

G. Busca, *Della Architettura Militare*, 60.

W. Braunfels. *Mittelalterliche Stadtbaukunst in der Toskana*, 47.

British Museum, London, 7, 8.

Centro di studi sui castelli, Montagnano, 43.

Chastillon. *Topographie Française*, 77.

Codex Cicogna. Museo Correr, Venice, 85.

Horst de la Croix, 27, 28, 44, 45, 46, 48, 49, 50, 51, 52, 53, 54, 57, 58, 59, 63, 64, 65, 67, 72, 73, 74, 79.

Foto Cartolibraria F. Boreggi, Cittadella, 42.

Foto CIM Combier Imprimeur Macon. Permission SPADEM 1969 by FRR: 89.

Foto Greff, SERP, Paris, 35.

Fotografia I. Milocco, Palmanova, 81.

Fototeca Unione, Rome, 16, 17, 20, 26, 29, 30, 33, 34.

Henri Frankfort. *Art and Architecture of the Ancient Orient*, 5, 6,

J. Hulot and G. Fougères. *Sélinonte: la ville, l'acropole et ses temples,* 18, 19.

F. Krischen. *Die Griechische stadt, wiederherstellungen*, 21, 22, 25.

A. W. Lawrence. *Greek Architecture*, 11.

B. Lorini. *Le fortification di B. Lorini*, 61.

A. Lupicini. *Della Architettura Militare*, 80.

Courtesy of Dott. Giovanni Martinelli, Mayor of Lucca, 71.

L. Mauceri. *Il castello Eurialo nella storia e nell'arte*, 15.

James Mellaart. *Çatal Hüyük*, 2, 3.

James Mellaart. *Earliest Civilizations in the Near East*, 1, 4.

Morini, 75.

Musee Vauban, Neuf Brisach, 90, 91.

National Library, Florence, 76

Courtesy of the Eugen Rentsch Verlag, Zurich, 88.

E. Rocchi. *Le Fonti Storiche dell'architettura Militare*, 62

Courtesy of Gen. Guilio Schmidt, Istituto geografica militare, Florence, 14.

Sopraintendenza ai Monumenti, Udine, 82.

Viollet-le-Duc. *An Essay on the Military Architecture of the Middle Ages,* 37, 38, 39, 40, 41, 55, 68.

Viollet-le-Duc. *La Cité de Carcassonne*, 35.

Armin von Gerkan. *Griechische Staedteanlagen*, 12, 13, 31.

Armin von Gerkan. *Die Stadtmauern*, 23, 24.

Zeiller. *Topographie*. 69.